Branding Your Business

THE SUNDAY TIMES

Branding Your Business

Promoting your business, attracting customers and standing out in the market place

James Hammond

KOGAN PAGE

London and Philadelphia

Publisher's note

Every possible effort has been made to ensure that the information contained in this book is
accurate at the time of going to press, and the publishers and author cannot accept responsibility
for any errors or omissions, however caused. No responsibility for loss or damage occasioned to
any person acting, or refraining from action, as a result of the material in this publication can be
accepted by the editor, the publisher or the author.

First published in Great Britain and the United States in 2008 by Kogan Page Limited

Apart from any fair dealing for the purposes of research or private study, or criticism or review,
as permitted under the Copyright, Designs and Patents Act 1988, this publication may only be
reproduced, stored or transmitted, in any form or by any means, with the prior permission in writing
of the publishers, or in the case of reprographic reproduction in accordance with the terms and
licences issued by the CLA. Enquiries concerning reproduction outside these terms should be sent
to the publishers at the undermentioned addresses:

120 Pentonville Road
London N1 9JN
United Kingdom
www.koganpage.com

525 South 4th Street, #241
Philadelphia PA 19147
USA

© James Hammond, 2008

The right of James Hammond to be identified as the author of this work has been asserted by him
in accordance with the Copyright, Designs and Patents Act 1988.

The views expressed in this book are those of the author, and are not necessarily the same as those
of Times Newspapers Ltd.

ISBN 978 0 7494 5073 1

British Library Cataloguing-in-Publication Data

A CIP record for this book is available from the British Library.

Library of Congress Cataloging-in-Publication Data

Hammond, James, 1952–
  Branding your business : promoting your business, attracting customers, and standing
out in the market place / James Hammond.
      p. cm.
  Includes bibliographical references and index.
  ISBN 978-0-7494-5073-1
  1. Branding (Marketing)--Management. 2. Consumer behavior. 3. Brand name
products--Psychological aspects. 4. Senses and sensation. 5. Communication in
marketing. I. Title.
  HF5415.1255.H36 2008
  658.8'27--dc22
                                                                2007047429

Typeset by JS Typesetting Ltd, Porthcawl, Mid Glamorgan
Printed and bound in India by Replika Press Pvt Ltd

Contents

Acknowledgements

If I took the space to thank all the friends, colleagues and associates who had made an impact on my almost 30 years in the advertising, marketing and branding profession, it would make a very long book in itself, but a boring time for the readers. Instead, I'd just like to express my deep gratitude to you all (you know who you are) and I hope that this book in some way reflects the knowledge and understanding I have gleaned from you during my career.

I must, however, single out some special people, without whose help this book could never have got off the ground. First, there is the great team at my publishers, Kogan Page, who were excited from day one about the subject and concept of the book. Thanks especially to Julia Swales and Annika Knight – you're both stars.

Thanks also to my good friend and Business Manager, Sarah Anderson, and to Dr Michael Yapko (Michael, you have helped me in more ways than you know).

Last, but by no means least, a very special thank you must go to my wife, Mary, herself a successful marketing and public relations consultant, for putting up with a grumpy old man for months on end as he struggled to complete the manuscript within the deadline.

(I would have mentioned my cats, Mr George and Tibbles, but they're too busy eating or sleeping to care either way.)

About the author

James Hammond has spent almost 30 years in advertising, marketing, design and branding. From his initial time as a graphic designer and copywriter, he progressed to heading up brand consultancies responsible for the brand management, sales and marketing, corporate identity and advertising for Top 100 companies including Yellow Pages, Virgin, Norwich Union, EMI and British Telecom.

James has also worked with numerous blue-chip organisations as an independent brand consultant, as well as helping smaller businesses and not-for-profits to strengthen their branding and profitability.

A well-seasoned speaker and presenter, James has conducted branding workshops, seminars and in-house training programmes throughout the United Kingdom. In 2001 he chaired and presented two key European conferences on Customer Care and Managing Change, attended by chief executives from major UK-based corporations.

In addition to his brand consultancy work, James is also a qualified psychotherapist. As James puts it, 'Understanding how people think is crucial to helping them as a therapist. But it's also one of the vital keys to knowing how to brand a business. Psychology is a rare ingredient in marketing, but it should really lead the way. My work as a therapist has greatly influenced my approach to branding.'

Visit the author's website at www.brandhalo.co.uk.

Introduction

I don't know what kind of business you own or manage. It could be that you're a sole proprietor looking to expand, but can't seem to generate the extra sales you need to take your business to the next level. You might be the marketing manager of a medium-sized enterprise that's struggling to keep the competition at bay, but have exhausted all promotional ideas and don't know what else to do. You could be a budding entrepreneur, keen to establish your own business – any kind of business – but don't know how to differentiate it from all the other, similar businesses out there. Perhaps you are a fundraiser in a not-for-profit organisation fighting for attention – maybe even survival – among the other 200,000-plus charities in the United Kingdom alone.

What I do know is that at some stage you'll probably have heard about the subject of branding. Given that most small business operators spend more time working in their business than on it, you might not have realised just how critical branding is to business success, but you knew that it warranted further investigation. So, like most small or medium-sized enterprise owners or managers, you ventured out to the bookstore ready to scour the shelves for helpful books on branding. What a surprise you may have met with.

It probably didn't take you long to realise that there are quite a few books out there that deal with the subject. The problem is, they're not talking to you. They're talking academically. Or theoretically. Or they're talking about specifics, like corporate identity, or website design, or how to write a 'killer' mission statement. Some might even venture to tell you that you need to 'get a brand' – but the chances are, they don't tell you how to do it.

Most of the time, the plethora of branding books are giving in-depth analyses of huge globe-circling conglomerates that make more money in one day than your current setup's been making in a year – perhaps 10 years.

The problem is, what works in mega-companies doesn't often translate well into the small business arena. Blue-chip tomes on strategic planning models along with corridors of brand research gurus – and the giga-budgets to go with them – are not the stuff smaller businesses can lay their hands on. (A small caveat here, though. In this book, I do refer to some big corporations by way of describing good brands. But not as a model for 'how to do it'; merely to show that it has been done.)

Yet it's the small to medium-sized business operator who needs brand help more than the rest. In the United Kingdom there are at the time of writing around 5 million small businesses in existence (defined as having up to 49 employees). In the United States, according to the 2005 figures from the Office of Advocacy there were nearly 30 million businesses in operation with up to 500 employees. Across the globe, small businesses are the lifeblood of the economy. So how come most of the branding books out there just don't address the problem, or make it more complicated than it needs to be?

Well, this book is different. It's written with the small to medium-sized organisation in mind. The whole book is based on a practical, no-nonsense, down-to-earth approach to a subject that is greatly misunderstood by the majority of businesses – especially the ones that think a brand is created behind closed doors in some navel-gazing brainstorming session. Or the unfortunate business owners duped into spending hard-earned cash to pay for a new logo or 'identity overhaul' before understanding that logos alone will not do the trick.

> **Branding is one of the hottest trends in business – and one of the most misunderstood.**
>
> **(Wall Street Journal)**

This book will explain, using a minimum of technical jargon, how to build a powerful brand by creating a Brand Halo™. It's the encapsulation of nearly 30 years' experience in the brand business, working with some of the biggest blue-chip organisations as well as the smallest of companies and charities, down to the one-person start-up. By the end of this book you will not only have the blueprint for a successful brand but will be able to identify areas of your business where you can begin immediately to put innovative, brand-building ideas into practice.

This is not a 'dip in, dip out' book. You need to start at the beginning and go through every chapter in turn systematically if you want to reap the benefits this book can bring. This is especially true if you have little or no understanding of the psychology of human behaviour, because, as you'll see, that is one of the most fundamental parts of building a brand. That's why a significant part of this book is devoted to explaining how customers think, and how they buy.

But here's a piece of friendly advice. Read this book as soon as you can. Do it before your competitor does. And do it before some design consultancy, advertising agency or marketing consultant comes along and persuades you that your brand needs a redesign, or a new advertising campaign, or a new marketing strategy. Don't misunderstand; all of these elements may well be very necessary in your business – but not until you fully appreciate what a brand is, and how to create your own.

In times past, marketing gurus would warn business owners like you and me that 'no customers means no business'. That statement is fast being replaced by 'no brand means no business', for the simple reason that if you don't have a brand, all you have is a commodity. And commodities don't command loyalty; they only focus on price. With Eastern countries like China and India becoming major players in the world's economy, businesses in the Western world are already finding it hard to compete in a purely price-based market.

> **The art of marketing is largely brand building. If not a brand, it will be viewed as a commodity.**
>
> **(Philip Kotler)**

Your business need not be concerned about competing on price if it has a strong brand. Research has consistently shown that customers will pay a premium for their preferred brand, especially if that brand has successfully gained their long-term loyalty.

In this brand-driven climate, traditional marketing techniques are no longer sufficient to create business success. Advertising is losing its pulling power. More direct mail is going straight in the waste-paper basket than ever before, and if traditional selling was only ever a 'numbers game', without a brand for support, its days are definitely numbered. Even the rise of technology-based customer care approaches, such as the once-hailed customer relationship management (CRM) systems, call centres and the like, have done little to aid business development. (Let's face it. When you're number 23 in a call-waiting queue and have been held there for 20 minutes, occasionally spoken to by some distorted, pre-recorded, unemotional voice telling you that 'your call is important to us', you get the feeling that someone somewhere has completely lost the plot, and has thrown any concept of building a strong brand out of the window.)

Yes, it's a scary time for your business if it's perceived more as *bland* than as *brand*. But this book can change all that for your business. And you don't need the deep pockets and huge resources of the blue-chip corporations to do it. In the following chapters you'll learn how to surround your business with a Brand Halo™ that will determine how every customer is treated, consistently and purposefully. You'll discover how a mixture of psychology and marketing can lay the foundations of a brand that truly exists in the only place where a brand can exist: *in the mind of the customer*.

Unlike many other books on branding, this one doesn't start by asking you where you are now with your brand and its various dynamics. The chances are, you don't really know. You're just aware that something needs to be done but you're not sure what it is. We have a fair bit to learn and understand first. Then, and only then, can we address what your brand needs to stand for, and how to communicate that to the customer. You'll need to ensure that some essentials are in place – such as making sure that your product or service has a clearly defined market. Or that you have the resources (or aim to acquire the resources) to see a brand-building exercise through. Even if you are only a very small operation at the moment, you'll need to spend time, effort and even some money on building your brand.

Of course, just how much you need to spend is something that I can't tell you, because it will vary considerably, depending on the kind of business you operate and what market you are addressing. I think you'd agree that if your brand is meant to convey professionalism and a powerful image, using scrap paper for your letterhead and the cut end of a potato to stamp your name and address on it (using some paint left over from redecorating the garden shed) probably won't be up to the mark.

I've read a great deal about bootstrapping – setting up your business with little or no money. I don't have a problem with that, especially if you are low on funds and you are aiming at a commodity market where a brand is of little value. However, if you want to create a sustainable and profitable brand, you need to appreciate this: *you might be able to bootstrap your start-up business, but you can't bootstrap your brand.*

On the other hand, there's little point in pouring money down the drain in advertising and sales promotion gimmicks or expensive collateral materials if they are not part of an overall brand approach.

With these things in mind, let's begin the process of creating a powerful brand for your business.

1

Nothing but the brand

Products are made in the factory, but brands are created in the mind.

Walter Landor

Just what is a brand, and who is the customer?

JUST WHAT IS A BRAND?

It's 8.30 am and I'm lacing up my Nike trainers ready for the morning jog. My Apple iPod is primed with a stash of Madonna tracks and there's a can of Coke at the ready for when the thirst hits.

In half an hour I'll be back. With my new Gillette shaver at the ready, I'll shower and then head for town. I've got some shopping to do before I board the Virgin plane taking me to my holiday destination that I booked through lastminute.com. I'll grab a burger for lunch in McDonald's or maybe just enjoy a coffee in Starbucks and eat later in Pizza Express.

One thing's for certain: by the end of the day, I'll be exposed to a multitude of companies and celebrities, each one vying for attention and yelling in my ear, 'Choose me, not her; choose us, not them.' Slogans, old and new, will tell me to 'just do it' as I run round the field, that 'I'm lovin' it' as I eat my burger or that the drink I've just downed is 'the real thing'.

What is it about these businesses that grabs my attention? Is it just the price of their goods or services? Is it the products themselves? The answer is a resounding 'no' on both counts. Some of these companies command a much higher price than their rivals, yet still outsell them every day. And the products are not always better quality – often it's the same product with just a different label, glued or stitched in place when the factory bell rings and the assembly line changes. Is there a massive difference between an iPod and every other MP3 player on sale? Not if it's just down to playing an MP3 track. How can Starbucks charge so much for coffee when if it's thirst you're looking to quench, you can buy a cup of tea or coffee at most petrol stations?

People are brands, too

And what about people like Madonna, Beckham and a host of other singers, sporting stars or media personalities? Is it just that they are great at what they do? Again, they may be good, but it would be foolish to think that there's never anyone with better skills or abilities out there. Is Madonna really the best singer in the whole wide world? No, but then, it doesn't really matter whether she is or she isn't.

The simple fact is, what makes them successful is not really down to tangible qualities at all. It's not what's in the can, or bottle, or cup. It's not the song, or how well it's sung. It's not the shoe and it's not the plane. Of course, every product or service must offer some kind of benefit, as we shall discover later. But benefits alone, in the way traditional marketing has understood them, are no longer sufficient to make something or someone stand out from the crowd. What makes these businesses and people powerful is that they are outstanding brands.

> **Be distinct or extinct.**
>
> **(Tom Peters,** *In Search of Excellence*)

Brands represent much more than a factual, rational connection to the product or service. They go beyond the boundaries of reason and extend into emotion. In 2003, researchers conducted a laboratory experiment based on the famous 'Pepsi Challenge', a long-running blind taste test where respondents were shown to prefer the taste of Pepsi to that of its rival, Coke. When asked to taste both Coca-Cola and Pepsi without the tasters knowing which brand was which, preference for the Pepsi taste scored higher than that for Coke. Yet when the tasters were told beforehand which one was Coca-Cola and which one was Pepsi, guess what happened? Three-quarters of the tasters declared their preference for Coca-Cola.

Logical? Reasonable? No way. But who said brands were about logic and rationality? Through magnetic brain scans, researchers found that the awareness of Coke as the drink they were tasting stimulated a part of the brain that had little to do with taste and a lot to do with memory and self-image. Quite literally, the Coke brand triggered a behaviour and response way beyond anything to do with the drink in the can.

Does the average person in the street really care that much about a soft drink? Consider this. In 1985, Coke decided to introduce a sweeter formula, called 'New Coke', to replace its tried and tested recipe. One would have expected consumers to greet the news with interest. Instead, public outrage at the very idea of changing Coke's formula became the subject of national debate. Less than 90 days after New Coke's multi-million-dollar launch, it was pulled off the shelves. Television programmes were interrupted to bring viewers the news, and in the US Senate, no less, Democratic senator David Pryor described it as 'a meaningful moment in US history'. Coke's capitulation was seen as a victory against those who wanted to destroy a national institution.

All that for a can of drink. Are you kidding? Well, for the sake of emphasis, let me repeat: it has not so much to do with the taste and a lot to do with the brand.

Don't give me facts... my mind's made up

But what about other purchases where taste isn't involved? Surely when we buy items such as cars, computers and clothes we're a little more logical and rational? Don't we rely on facts and figures to inform our purchasing habits?

The truth is, we might think that we buy goods or services only on the basis of data and information, but we'd be wrong. We are overloaded with information. We are given conflicting opinions from even the most distinguished experts on an almost daily basis. Our homes are the recipients of several hundred television and radio channels, the internet is heading rapidly to somewhere in the region of 50 billion web pages and our newsagents will have a choice of over 8,000 magazine titles with which to tempt us.

In our fast-paced, hectic, stress-filled lives, how can we possibly make any kind of logical decisions about anything? We can't. We were stricken with 'analysis paralysis' some time ago, and now we exhibit the uncomfortable after-effects of absorbing information and data that are in conflict. Is red wine good for your heart if you drink it regularly... or is it bad? (Replace the drinking of wine with the eating of chocolate and ask the same question.) Is depression caused by a chemical imbalance or is it about life management? Is a high-fat diet bad, or should we actually eat more protein? How much liquid should we drink each day, and does it have to be water? Is global warming a reality or just an opinion from some alarmists? Can you trust any information? With scandals such as Enron still ringing in our ears, can a business be relied upon to provide true accounts of its product or service?

At the end of the day, the frustration, confusion and mistrust people experience has led to the one single source of decision making that can be relied upon: people's own feelings about the issue. It won't just depend on the latest research report or the peer-group recommendation. It won't even be done at a totally conscious level.

But one thing is certain. The brand – whatever it is, wherever it's from – will be a major factor in that decision process.

The brand is centre stage. It's the all-singing, all-dancing set of emotional characteristics that prod, cajole and play with your senses – repeated, replicated, duplicated and pushed at you, determined to carve a niche, find a place, open a filing cabinet and create a spot, however tiny it may be, in the part of our neural network we've come to know as long-term memory. That's why a brand resides in the mind, not in the factory or showroom.

Yes, folks, in the society of today it's the brand, the whole brand and nothing but the brand. In the 21st century, just about everything is a brand! And if you want to survive in business, or stand any chance of growing your company to the dizzy heights of some of the corporates I've mentioned, you'd better get rid of the bland and replace it with the brand. Because, as sure as Beanz Meanz Heinz, without a strong brand you're dead in the water.

Branding brings benefits

Get it right, however, and you can enjoy the tremendous benefits that a powerful brand can bring: like increased sales (or, in the case of a charity, increased donations and gifts from supporters), maximum exposure and awareness of your product or service, a loyal and long-term customer base, perhaps even premium pricing, depending upon the market you're in. And last, but by no means least, dedicated employees who come to work because they understand the brand, believe in it and feel a part of it. (For example, many of the innovative elements of Virgin's operations have originated from staff concepts and ideas – something positively encouraged by the organisation and by founder Richard Branson, himself a powerful brand.)

That's not all. When your brand is strong, it's actually worth something and becomes part of the intellectual property on your balance sheet. Valuation of brands as intangible assets has become a major area of focus for investors and shareholders. In 2005, for example, Interbrand/Business Week estimated the value of Coca-Cola's brand (no, not the drink, or the bottling plants or the office furniture) to be a staggering $67.5 billion! By the time this book is published, it may well be that Microsoft has easily exceeded that valuation.

How on earth did we arrive at this spot today where the power and potential of a brand can either make or break a business? Let's take a quick look at the development of branding and realise that much of what companies have claimed as their brand has, in fact, been totally misunderstood.

A brand? It's nothing but a pain in the backside

The meaning of the word 'brand' can be traced back to ancient Greek and Roman times. But perhaps the meaning we know best refers to the branding used by cowboys in the days of the Wild West to denote ownership of livestock.

Ranchers would take an iron rod which had affixed to it at one end an iron plate bearing a symbol of their ranch, or the initials of the ranch owner. They would heat this branding iron in the campfire to glowing point. This iron would then be applied on to the backside hip of a rancher's animal – literally burned into the skin – in order to aid identification and deter cattle or horse rustling.

In effect, it was a one-sided deal. The rancher identified the animal as his, but all the cow or horse got out of it was a pain in the backside. Sadly, if we liken this situation to the modern world, many businesses are repeating the same relationship. Companies often think of a brand merely as a way of showing ownership from a visual basis. Vast sums of money – more than a small business can usually afford – are wasted on having elaborate logos designed and produced, or mission statements written and placed in expensive frames in the boardroom. At the same time, the customer gets poor service and poor value – and the company's brand is merely a painful experience for the recipient. It's that kind of enterprise that's doomed to failure.

An emphasis on identity

When industrialisation took place in the 19th century, the definition of a brand was still one of identification. Products that had been made in the local communities, such as household items like detergents, were now being produced and packaged by factories, yet they were still trying to sell their goods to a customer base that had previously purchased the locally made versions. In order to compete against the more familiar local products, companies started applying identifying signs to the packaging. This practice developed into what we now call trademarks. By the early 20th century these logos were being accompanied by billboard advertising, slogans and radio commercials. The word 'brand' started to encompass both visual and promotional characteristics.

When the focus shifted more towards the customer in the mid-1990s, the meaning of 'brand' expanded once again. With an emphasis on 'delivering the promise to the customer', companies began to develop elaborate plans, promising to 'delight' the customer, or 'wow' the customer. Companies drew up mission statements aimed at showing the world just how wonderful and sincere they were in their commercial objectives. Marketing consultancies pushed for what they called 'integrated communications', referring to the need for a company's marketing campaigns and collateral to be coordinated in such a way that a seamless presentation throughout every nook and cranny of the business was generated. Oh dear, wrong again.

The brand landscape of today

So where are we now? Has the expanded meaning of 'brand' led to a new wave of highly successful small and medium-sized businesses with powerful brands? Sadly, no. At the time of writing, business failures are at an all-time high, and with the increased competition of global enterprise, unless the approach to building a brand is understood from a different perspective, change is unlikely to occur.

In the 21st century we've witnessed change in just about every aspect of life. And when it comes to products and services, the future looks grim for those businesses hoping to hold on to customers in a commodity market where the only loyalty is to the vendor with the lowest price. Unfortunately, that's where a great many markets are heading. Products and services are often so similar that there's no point in spending time reading specifications in order to decide which one to choose. And don't expect the customer service experience behind them to bear any worthwhile fruit. You and I both know that customer care is pathetic at the best of times. It's fronted either by bureaucrats, robots or, frankly my dear, people who don't give a damn. Well, all I can say is, they will. It's only a matter of a few years before the realisation that customers have deserted the sinking ship and sought another place in which to spend their money on the things they enjoy. It's called *Brandland*. And they're heading for its city centre.

Defining a brand

So, as we prepare to create a powerful brand for your business, let's be clear about our definition of a brand:

A brand is not a logo. A brand is not a slogan. A brand is not an identity, corporate or otherwise. A brand is not a symbol or a shape.

It's not mailshots, mission statements or mantras. It's not colours, credos or calling cards.

A brand is not a set of meaningless gimmicks, such as everyone wearing 'have a nice day' badges or answering calls with a stupid phrase or statement.

It's not even about having 'all your ducks in a row'. The idea that any business has to look and operate exactly the same in every single aspect of its operation is not only unnecessary but nigh on impossible. (I've never consulted for a business where Accounts Receivable had the remotest interest in what colour the next sales brochure was going to be, or why their room was going to be repainted in the same shade.)

And contrary to what some so-called brand experts tell you, it's not a promise you make to your customer. At best, all any company can do is try. But promise? You've got to be kidding. Promises can be broken; most of the time they are. And when that happens regularly, the brand suffers, often irrevocably. (What's even crazier is the idea of making a promise and then rewarding the customer when you break it. Concepts like 'we promise to do such and such or your

> money back' are a basic contradiction in terms. If you promise to do something, you should do it. And if you can't... then don't promise it in the first place.)

In fact, a brand isn't even something that you or your business owns! Rather:

> A brand is the total sensory experience a customer has with your company and its product or service.

A brand is an experience that's embedded in the mind of every person who has ever come into contact with your staff and your product or service. That, my friends, is how it is. And if that customer experience doesn't match the way your company describes its brand, or thinks about its brand, then guess what – you lose!

Please don't misunderstand. I'm not saying that logos, advertising campaigns, mission statements, colours and the like aren't important. They can be vital parts of the brand experience your customers have. At the same time, it's important to notice the emphasis on who gets to determine what's important and what isn't. That's right, the customer. Put customers first and work on how to develop the best rapport; then you can go to town on creating brand impact with all the tools available, from logos to colour schemes. The trouble is, most small businesses work the wrong way round, focusing first on designing symbols or corporate identities before understanding their place in the whole brand scheme. I call such folly 'cart-before-horse-ism' (see Figure 1.1).

WHO IS THE CUSTOMER?

All this talk about customers. But who are the customers of today, and how are they different from those of bygone days?

Today's customer has been through an enormous change process that began at the start of the 20th century. Since that time, huge advances in technology, communication and information have given everyone in the Western world

Illustration by Claire Macdonald

Figure 1.1   Cart-before-horse-ism

a variety of choices and options never before available. We live in an age of abundance and surplus, at least in the Western world. But this supersaturation of products has created a commoditisation of markets that once upon a time could bawl out their claims of 'differentiation', whether it be in quality, features, functionality or benefits. Today, many markets are a collection of 'me-too' products and services, offering the same stuff at the same price by the same methods using the same technology.

Surprisingly, most marketing approaches fashioned in another era still continue to be used, despite their out-of-date (and in some cases erroneous) reasoning. In the late 1900s, when door-to-door salesman had their heyday in selling everything from vacuum cleaners to hair restorers, a salesman by the name of Elmo St Louis wrote a theory on how advertising worked. This theory developed over time into a sales approach known as the 'hierarchy of effects' – designed to help salespeople create a greater number of sales successes. The idea behind the approach was that people purchased goods and services in a straightforward, linear, thinking manner. That is, customers became aware of the goods and what they could do, mainly through advertising or some other sales communication. The customer would then become interested in them, which in turn created a desire for the product, leading to a purchase.

Simple, eh? But hopelessly off track. By the early 1960s, several different versions of this model had been constructed, one of the most popular among sales and marketing people being the A-I-D-A approach, which stood for

Attention, Interest, Desire, Action. Other refinements followed, including modifying the mnemonic to become A-I-D-C-A, the additional 'C' standing for Conviction.

The problem is, this model, like other outdated ideas, fails to understand how the mind works in making decisions. As we'll see, making your mind up about whether or not to buy a product or service is not a simple 'I'm interested so I'll buy' process. Nor does A-I-D-A take into account the various psychological influencers of our decision-making process – the very elements that help create that picture of our favourite brands in our mind's eye.

Also in the 1960s, E Jerome McCarthy came up with the '4 Ps' of marketing (price, product, promotion and place). Essentially, this concept argued that the key to business success was simply to supply the right product at the right price in the right place using the right promotion. It was a model that, during those years of mass production, became extremely popular. Over the years, more 'Ps' have been added (one of the first being people, followed by issues such as performance, profit and almost any other word that begins with a 'P' that has something to do with business). Again, this is an out-of-date model because, as Gareth Morgan (1988) states, 'it unconsciously emphasizes the inside-out view (looking from the company outwards), whereas the essence of marketing should be the outside-in approach'. That's why I prefer to call the '4 Ps' the '4 RIPs'; they're dead, because they simply don't cut it any more.

Post-modernist thinking has eroded the former beliefs in absolutes, and society has been reshaped as a result into interpretations of what the world means to us on an individual basis.

Brands are the express checkout for people living their lives at ever-increasing speed.

(Brandweek)

The pace of life is much quicker, too. Author Agnieszka Winkler emphasised in her book *Warp Speed Branding: The impact of technology on marketing* (1999), 'We are living in a sliver of time during which 10 years has redefined the concept of fast food from a drive-thru McDonald's to a 30-second microwave meal; nail polish dries in 30 seconds; photos are developed in one hour; and money comes out of street corner machines instantly.'

This is a 'need-to-stay-in-touch' society, where estimates suggest that by 2010, 90 per cent of the world will own a mobile phone. Already, 50 per cent of children in the United States have mobile phones, a figure that is also set to rise rapidly over the next few years.

We live on borrowed money, with credit card debt at an all-time high. In the United Kingdom, at the time of writing, there are more credit cards than people. As the rock group Queen sang, 'I want it all'. And if the money isn't there, they'll borrow it, often wildly exceeding their ability to pay it back. But paying it back is about tomorrow, so why worry when you can have what you want today?

Yes, consumers don't just want it all, they want it now. It's the age of immediacy and least effort for most gain. Witness the rise of the health and fitness market, where gymnasiums and health clubs woo their audience with the promise of a body to die for, if only you can commit to a regular workout. That's often too much to ask. A significant number of subscribers to health club memberships will make only a few trips in any given year and may even abandon the hard physical activity after the first session.

Still, if you can't manage a workout, you can always avail yourself of every conceivable type of diet, whether it's based on fish, meat or some rare and unpronounceable herb. That's if you have the time to prepare such dishes. If not, don't worry. There is a plethora of low-fat, low-calorie microwaveable meals out there to save you the hassle. And if their small portion offerings cause you to crave for more food than your diet sheet allows, there are always the appetite-depressant pills to help you say 'no'. Interesting, then, at the same time as the body beautiful becomes almost an obsession, the rise in global obesity has been described as a 'time bomb' and a 'global epidemic' with serious consequences for world health in the coming decade.

The changing face of the customer

Yes, a great deal has changed as far as your customers are concerned. No longer are they the stereotypical folks that live on the hill, woman at home keeping the house and looking after the kids while hubby is out working in a job he'll have for life. Instead, single-parent families, same-sex partnerships and multiple relationships are often the norm of society today – and who has a job for life any more? What's more, trust in the once-held-in-awe institutions has long gone. Authorities, politicians and even religious figures are treated with suspicion amid stories of sleaze, deceit and betrayal.

All this has created a 'new' customer for whom traditional marketing has little or nothing to offer. Sales and marketing commentators would once state, 'the customer is king', as though the world consisted of customers served by their favourite company in a pleasant little relationship that would last for ever. Today, the customer has moved way beyond this limited view. The king has been joined by the queen and both have become supreme dictators – demanding, forceful, low on loyalty and high on self.

The point is, your customer today is calling the shots. She or he has heard it all before and doesn't give a care about your banal and totally dismissive claim of 'exceptional customer service', because that's a given today, not a bonus – even though very few businesses ever live up to their self-indulgent assertions.

That's why the customer is no longer moved by meaningless soundbites, straplines or empty phrases such as 'We're unique', 'Our product's unique', 'We're different because of our people', 'Become our customer... you'll be glad you did', 'No... we really ARE different...', 'Quality, service... and much, much, more'.

Blah, blah, blah...

The two keys of branding

But wait a moment. If the picture really is that bad (and I sure hope I've shown that it is very, very bad), and if customers control and create the brand through their own experience, then what control do you have over ensuring that they see your business in the best possible light? If it isn't logos, slogans, adverts or promises, what is it?

The answer is in two parts. The first has to do with you. It's about having a different mindset about your business and what it needs to do to win and keep customers. It's about understanding that a brand is not only about customers' heads but about their hearts too. It means changing your position from seeing a brand as a collection of isolated activities, to seeing your brand as a holistic experience for the customer, one built in to all the important places the customer defines as reflections of your business and what it stands for. In short, it's about looking through the window as a customer, rather than looking out as a business owner. Then, and only then, can you begin to appreciate the second part: influence.

That's right, influence. Influence your customers' experiences of your business. If you don't want to drown in a commodity pit, influence is really all you have to build a brand. But the good news is, it's all you need. And it ain't rocket science.

The all-encompassing Brand Halo™

You can have a major influence over your customers' perception of your brand by creating what I call a Brand Halo™. A Brand Halo™ may well include most of the components mentioned earlier: logos, mission statements, slogans and the like. But unlike the fragmented, empty purpose most of these elements provide when used in isolation, this time they'll be a part of an overall dialogue with the customer that only stops when you can no longer be bothered to have something to say.

> In my time presenting branding seminars, I've stayed in all kinds of hotels. Sadly, I've experienced many where at one time the owners would gaze proudly upon the beautiful décor and highly polished surroundings, nodding at smiling staff in neatly pressed uniforms ushering people to their rooms with an air of enthusiasm and motivation. I've been back five years later, only to find the paint peeling, the carpet threadbare and staff with an attitude that sucks. But I guess you can't blame them. They've seen the writing on the wall. It's in huge bold lettering and the message is 'it's downhill all the way', so why bother being nice to guests? For whatever reason, the owners stopped talking to the customers. Or maybe they still spoke, but the only point they made – repeatedly – is 'we don't care any more'.

A Brand Halo™ fits right around your company and displays what you have to offer in the best possible light. If it's polished correctly, you'll have a strong brand. If it's tarnished, guess what... your days in business could be numbered.

What's more, it really doesn't matter whether you market a product or a service; whether you're selling canned drinks, running a hairdressing salon or providing financial services to your clients. Any manufacturer or service provider can build a strong brand.

Sodium chloride, basic table salt, is a commodity – and one that presumably can't be improved upon in any meaningful way. So you'd think there'd be little that could be done to turn it into a brand, wouldn't you? Wrong. In North America, Morton Salt is one of the most respected and long-serving brands (it's been around since 1848). Such is its brand loyalty that of every two packs of salt sold, one is the Morton product. If that's not impressive enough, Morton Salt sells at a 20 per cent price premium above its competition! And all because of the emotive story they created of a little girl walking home from a store in the rain, holding an umbrella in one hand and a packet of Morton salt in the other. The pack was tilted back with the spout open and salt running out. The visual, of course, was to show that Morton salt wouldn't stick in the container in wet weather. This was accompanied by the slogan 'When It Rains, It Pours.' Today, additives enable all salt brands to flow freely, so you can't even attribute Morton's market share to product differentiation. The fact is, Morton is the preferred brand because of what it means in the mind of the consumer.

'But', you protest, 'I'm in a business-to-business market. I don't just sell to one person, I have to persuade various executives throughout an organisation.' So what? All this means is that you have to influence more people at the same time. But whatever position they occupy in that company you're going after, they are still all human beings influenced by emotions, feelings and rapport. Believe me, branding is not exclusive to the business-to-consumer market, even though some of the parameters may be different in that market. Even a not-for-profit organisation can construct a powerful brand by using the Brand Halo™ approach in this book.

A brand of EPIC™ proportions

Your Brand Halo™ will be built upon four core components. They're easy to remember if you use the mnemonic EPIC™ (Figure 1.2):

E – stands for EMOTION. This is the key part of creating your powerful brand, and on it everything else will be built. If you don't have emotion as an ingredient in your product or service, you don't have a brand, you have a commodity.

P – stands for PERCEPTION. Emotions aren't stirred or influenced by thin air. They are the result of sensory stimulation arriving at the brain through the five senses: sight, sound, smell, taste and touch. Most small businesses focus only on the 'sight' sense, ignoring the power of the other four to really build a strong perception of the brand in the customers' minds.

I – stands for INNOVATION. Being aware of the five senses is one thing. Coming up with novel ways of presenting sensory information is something else. This is where your Brand Halo™ becomes your guiding light. All the important processes, systems and procedures will be documented in your Brand Halo™ manual, and employees will be given guidance on how to monitor and improve each customer Brand Reflection. Innovation is what keeps the brand alive and kicking. It gives longevity to an otherwise stagnant and outdated brand, and provides the freshness needed to keep your brand 'top of mind' when it comes to purchasing your type of product or service.

C – stands for COMMUNICATION. Why do you want to create an emotional brand? What is your purpose – and why should your customers or supporters care, anyway? This is where your Brand Storybook™ comes into play. Using narratives that describe your business along with your aims and achievements, you can communicate emotional messages to your customers and your staff and use them to underpin the whole customer experience.

Brands, like growth, are not static. You can't just create your brand and leave it alone. People change. Society changes. Even cultural biases change. And if your brand is to reflect the kind of image that says, 'we know, we understand, we're with you', then it needs to be continually polished. Through your Brand Halo™, built on the solid foundations outlined in this book, you can build a brand of EPIC™ proportions.

Figure 1.2 Your EPIC™ brand

Branding: not a cover-stick for a spotty business

A brand is not a short-term solution to building a business; it's a way of creating long-term competitive advantage. If you can add value through a strong brand, your future income streams will be more secure. Your customers will keep coming back for more and you can capitalise on their support and their enthusiasm to buy from you and your loyal and motivated workforce. This in turn means that you can provide a solid strategic base from which to develop new products and services, as well as plan for expansion and growth.

The fact that eight out of ten new businesses fail within the first year or so indicates that there are often some serious problems arising when would-be businesspeople attempt to set up and run a company. While this is a book about branding rather than business planning, it's important therefore to have an honest appraisal of where your business stands right now.

My assumption is that most of you reading this book operate a business that you want to expand and grow. Or, as an entrepreneur, you want to start a new enterprise that is also destined for growth. If yours is a not-for-profit organisation, you want to increase the number of supporters (particularly those who donate money) so that you can undertake important projects that resources don't permit at this moment in time.

In all of these cases, as I've said, a strong brand is essential for success. But branding is not a substitute for a solid business plan, or something to mask a poorly run operation. In the hands of a business owner without sufficient business acumen to understand the essentials of business – finance, planning, management, etc – heading down the branding trail can be a costly and disastrous exercise, and one that could so easily put a number of nails in the business coffin when focus on other fundamental business areas might have saved the day. As someone so eloquently said, you can put lipstick on a pig... but it's still a pig.

So let's establish a key prerequisite of creating a strong brand.

> There is a clearly defined market for your product or service.

OK, I know this sounds crazy. But too many business owners fall in love with their product or service offering and in doing so fail to appreciate that the market is either too small to expand in, or it's misunderstood, in the sense that it's not really where you belong. In other words, it's a case not just of identifying a market opportunity but also of asking if it's the right opportunity. Branding hasn't replaced the need for a target market to aim at; it's just redefined the parameters and approach. Here are some key points to think about:

- Is your product or service already in demand? What's the current state of the market: is it in decline, or is it a growth market? How much of it do you own? What research have you carried out to help indicate where your future market potential might be in, say, five or ten years' time? A brand does not create a market. *A brand gives you the most powerful weapon available to address the market – one that is already in existence, or one that your data have shown you is emerging in which there will be sufficient buyers for you to establish a profitable business.*

- How many competitors are you aware of that provide the same service or product as you? Do they dominate your market, and if so... why? What other products or services do they offer? How many do you offer and are they 'me-too' products pitched against those of your competitors? Do your competitors already have a powerful brand? If they do, chances are it's been built up over a period of time. It doesn't mean you can't build a better, stronger brand. But it may mean that your stamina and endurance will be put to the limit as you go past catch-up phase and into the lead. But don't get me wrong. The focus shouldn't just be on your competition, and sometimes small businesses can become paranoid about what their competitors are up to. A well-known saying in the horse-racing industry given as advice to jockeys is 'Keep your eyes on the finish line, not on the horse and rider by your side.' *A brand can help you exploit a competitor's weakness – but can the competitor exploit yours more?*

- If you are an entrepreneur, can you create a *sustainable* demand for your proposed offering? Have you paid attention to the shifting dynamics of society and culture, and important trends that will have a significant effect on the business of tomorrow? Witness the demise of the Polaroid instant camera. In the 1970s, being able to take a picture and have it emerge, fully developed, straight out of the camera was something quite innovative. But by the 1980s, high-street processing outlets were already offering one-hour turnaround on film processing from standard 35mm cameras, with better quality. In turn, the arrival of digital cameras that could take excellent pictures capable of being e-mailed across the globe seriously eroded the film processing industry. Now, most modern mobile phones have the ability to take a picture (or short video) and send it via the mobile phone network, dispensing with the need to involve a PC. Just because your idea seems great to you, that doesn't mean sufficient numbers of people will think the same over time. *You can't build a brand on a dream. But then again, you can't build a brand without one.*

- Are you a not-for-profit? If so, where does your organisation fit into the need you are attempting to address? How many other third-sector players are involved in the same issues as you? Where are the overlaps and places or issues upon which you might even compete? In the United Kingdom there have been instances in the past where lack of cooperation between similar charitable organisations not only led to duplication but also created instances of indiscriminate giving. Recognising this, some charities have merged, the result being an organisation capable of better service delivery, working to a much more focused purpose and one that can be justified to the target audience. *A brand cannot be used to defend confusion, fragmentation or unnecessary overlap in a not-for-profit sector.*

2

Understanding emotion

People don't ask for facts in making up their minds. They would rather have one good, soul-satisfying emotion than a dozen facts.

Robert Keith Leavitt

Branding the heart as well as the head

If you're not a fan of psychology, then you may struggle with this chapter. But hang in there, because this is the most important topic in the book. I'll try to keep it simple, but the fact is, if you don't understand what's being said here, you'll never create a powerful brand.

Marketing has developed as a discipline over the years but still tends to focus more on the head than on the heart of the customer. In fact, most marketers have little, if any, training in psychology or consumer behaviour of the kind needed to understand the customer of today.

Marketers and business owners fail to appreciate the one critical factor in building a brand today, and it's this:

> All brand purchases are emotional, because all brands are emotional.

Now, don't get me wrong. I'm not saying that you completely disregard every bit of common sense when you buy your new high-definition, flat-screen, surround-sound television. But if we're honest, lurking somewhere in that brain of yours are emotions such as *desire*, *want*, perhaps even *lust*. C'mon, don't deny it. You really wanted that all-singing, all-dancing television, didn't you? And once you'd bought it, you'd find any number of reasons to justify why you did it. 'Well, the other set was getting old. The picture wasn't sharp any more. There was a funny smell coming from the back.' You know what I mean.

The fact is, whether the purpose is to support a worthy cause or to buy your preferred make of toilet tissue, logic doesn't drive the purchasing process. Emotion does. Mr Spock might have lived his Vulcan life by reason and logic, but for us humans it's emotion underpinning and driving our decisions all the way.

When you are building a brand, emotion needs to be generated in two specific areas. The first is regarding your actual product or service; the second is regarding the customer experience of your whole operation. In other words, it's everything in your business that the customer deems important.

Let's be clear, though. Sometimes you might read an article (or even a book) on branding that talks only about the emotional side of the company as if the rational or logical side wasn't important at all. That's crazy! Although brands are emotional, logic and rationality still play a part. If I'm buying a new car, my emotions will influence me to select a brand that meets my emotional needs. But I still need to be assured that it has four wheels and an engine. And if that engine has something special about it, then however data or fact based, that feature may well add to my emotional connection with the brand. That's why, as we'll see shortly, we need to be clear about just what emotional benefit we're going to hang our brand on.

Think about the Coca-Cola and Pepsi taste test covered earlier. If the part of the brain creating a preference for Coke wasn't the area that was concerned about taste – a purely rational like/dislike decision – but was more about self-image, then what we're really saying is that the preference has materialised out of an emotional driver, not just a rational one. It's about how you and I *feel* about something, the structures we put in place in our minds that create *brand desire*. And it's all built around emotion. But that doesn't mean I completely disregard the taste, does it? If a drink tastes like bilge water, chances are I won't want to swallow even a drop.

Defining emotions

What exactly do we mean when we use the word 'emotion' and where does it fit into our decision-making process?

Understanding of how the brain works has developed in leaps and bounds in the past 50 or so years, and with the advent of such things as MRI brain scanning technology we are much better placed than formerly to appreciate how the brain processes both rational and emotional thoughts.

Suffice it to say that emotions, as far as branding is concerned, are a set of psychological structures, or frames of reference, formed and shaped in the mind and triggered by certain experiences. To some neuroscientists, emotions are distinct from feelings, in the sense that emotions are the generators for feelings. For the purposes of this book, however, I'm going to refer to emotions and feelings as the same desired outcome. As we shall see, one of the key requirements for building a brand that's ahead of the rest is to identify and influence emotional triggers in the purchasing process that create positive feelings about the product or service.

Two pathways to purchasing

Out of all the complex studies of neural pathways, chemicals and processing systems the brain consists of, one piece of knowledge we know about the brain's functioning is that there are basically two kinds of information being processed: *rational* and *emotional* (see Figure 2.1).

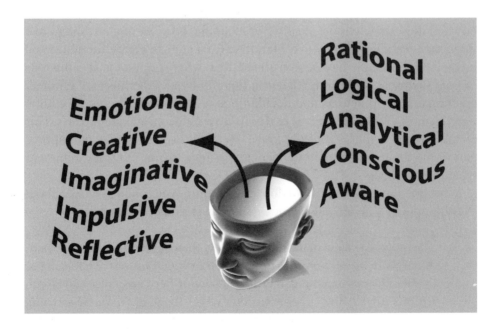

Figure 2.1   The two pathways of thinking

Old theories divided the processing of these different information types into a left-brain and a right-brain operation, the left brain being the dominant of the two, responsible for processing language, data, facts and figures – the 'logical' side, if you like – while the right brain was the more intuitive part, processing feelings, emotions and senses. Many neuroscientists now believe that both types of information are processed simultaneously as part of a total mechanism involving lots of crossover networks and sharing of information.

But here's the key point about this processing activity. The rational pathways progress information in a linear manner, one piece after the other. The emotional pathways, however, process data in parallel paths. So, this faster route doesn't connect information in a *logical* way; it relies on the rational brain parts to do that on its behalf. And, as studies show, the emotional structures that manage our emotional responses and connect them to the part of the brain that controls our thoughts and ultimate actions are wider and stronger than the pathways in the rational processing system. In other words, the *emotive* part of the brain is always one step ahead of the logical, rational part in processing information. Can you see where we're going with this?

Along with this rational/emotional circuitry, a little almond-shaped cluster (one on each side of the brain) known as the amygdala has a huge role to play in emotional processing. Not only does it involve itself in determining how emotions play out physically (for example, how we might respond to a threat or even a very funny joke) but it's also a storage centre for emotional memories. Research has demonstrated that when high-arousal situations present themselves, the amygdala can literally bypass the 'normal' rational/emotional brain functions and decide upon a response all by itself, calling upon its most vivid memories as part of its own decision-making process. This all takes place in literally milliseconds – without even involving the rational part of the brain and without the person having any conscious awareness of what's taken place!

What does any of this have to do with branding, you might ask? Just about everything. Let's understand some key points relating to brands:

■ The rational system of the brain is slower than its emotional counterpart. As a result, *our actions are determined by our emotions.* That is not to dismiss the rational mind; it is the connection between cause and effect. But it's always the support system, never the lead. *To build a strong brand, don't completely dismiss data such as product features, service options and, yes, even price.* Get your functional systems sorted out.

Just don't make their details the only aspect of your brand. Instead, translate their physical values into emotional connections you make with your customers. *People buy on emotion and justify with reason.*

- The emotional system of the brain is more powerful than the rational system. Conscious thoughts, however logical and rational, will always lead to an emotional outcome. Thoughts can also be irrational, as in the case of phobias, but they still lead to strong emotional outcomes – in this case, wholly negative ones. *To build a strong brand, you need to focus your attention on influencing as many positive emotions of your customer as you can, as often as you can.*

- Some parts of the emotional system operate beneath our conscious awareness, driven by memories of past associations and experiences. The process is immensely powerful, sometimes triggering actions over which we feel we have no control. *To build a strong brand, you need to create customer experiences that will become part of the customer's long-term memory store.* Put it this way: if customers are going to do something on the spur of the moment (like buy 1,000 widgets from you when they only planned to buy 3), let it be because of prior positive experiences you planted in their memory.

- The memory system of the brain responds more to past experiences that are specific and detailed rather than vague or fragmented. The stronger the emotional memory, the greater justification and reasoning will be used by the rational mind to support the outcome. *To build a strong brand, your customer experiences should exceed the already-determined expectations of your customers and evoke strong memories.* Of course, bad customer experiences (which we all have to live through on a regular basis, it seems) will also reside in memory. If that negative memory is strong, it's about all I need to decide not to do business with you.

How many emotions are there?

I've used the word 'emotion' many times already in this chapter. How many emotions exist? Antonio R Damasio MD, a behavioural neurologist and neuroscientist, suggests that there are six universal emotions: happiness, sadness, fear, anger, surprise and disgust.

Along with these six main feelings are secondary emotions such as embarrassment, jealousy, guilt or pride. Damasio also lists 'background emotions' such as well-being or malaise, being full of energy or being down, being enthusiastic, having anticipation or having dread. Unlike the other emotions, which are triggered by external factors, these are generated from within our own minds. Just as our main emotions can influence what we buy and how we buy it, these can all have a significant effect on our purchasing habits, too.

A famous advertising copywriter, Jerry Della Femina, once wrote an advertisement for a haemorrhoid cream supplier that said, 'If you've got a dollar, and you've got piles, send me your dollar and we'll get rid of your piles. Or, you can keep your dollar and keep your piles.' Now that's what I call black and white emotional options: pleasure or pain; the choice is yours.

When it comes to generating emotions about our business and our brand, we need to create positive feelings. If a customer has experienced a negative emotion as a result of how she has been treated, or let down by a product's performance, this may become an anchor in her emotional memory store that is triggered every time the business, product or service is being considered. Depending on how strong that anchor is, it may take considerable effort on the part of the company to turn this negative emotional anchor into a positive one. That may sound like common sense. But how many business owners really focus on generating positive emotional experiences for their customers – and potential customers – and do it regularly? Yet it can't be stated often enough that gaining emotional commitment from those who purchase your goods or services is the crucial factor for building a strong brand – not just for today but for the entire future of the brand.

Imagine you are at an airport, and over the tannoy system comes the announcement, 'We are sorry to announce that flight 1234 to Barbados is cancelled.' What is your immediate emotional reaction? Would you remember this scene the next time you planned to book a flight with an airline? Would it affect your decision as to which airline to fly with on subsequent trips? What do you make of the word 'sorry' in the announcement? Does its inclusion make you feel emotionally more understanding towards the airline? Or do you internalise it as just another empty word that isn't really meant by the company and certainly not by the person who said it? Does it shape how you feel about flying in general? Does it create in you an emotional anchor – a negative thought pattern – about that experience and that particular airline? Chances are it will – and most likely be added to that cute little amygdala's storehouse of retained memories.

So how will you, as a customer, deal with it? How do you want the airline to deal with it? How can they reverse the negative emotion you're feeling and turn it into a positive one? Was the tannoy system the best way to announce the cancellation? Should the word 'sorry' have been used at all? Would another word have been better?

And consider this: what if it was *your* airline company that cancelled the flight, your member of staff who had to break the bad news and your script that was being read out? How would you have handled it? What would you put in place – if anything – to try to win back some of your brand polish that's just become mightily tarnished? (Incidentally, here's one way that's guaranteed to screw the situation up even more, alienate people and give them indigestion all at the same time: offer them a discount voucher on a drink or sandwich while they wait for the next flight, if there is one. In the context of the scenario you've just read, wouldn't that be the craziest thing you could possibly do to people? It would? Then how come that's a typical response made by airlines when their flights are cancelled?)

As you can see, there are many emotional issues to consider about branding that are usually totally overlooked, even though there may be a pristine copy of the company's mission statement hanging proudly on the boardroom wall as customer chaos ensues.

Features...

With emotion being such a vital element to be addressed and understood, it's unfortunate that small businesses regularly make the mistake of promoting their product's or service's features to the customer, but leave out the emotional benefits.

What do I mean by 'features'? Marketing expert Philip Kotler says that features are 'characteristics that supplement the product's basic function'. In other words, features are attributes of a business, service or product. They are, in essence, what a thing does, rather than what the customer benefits from. They will also include the physical components, dimensions, colours and shapes of a product. In the case of a service, they will include the 'hard' systems and processes used in the delivery of the service, such as logistics, order processing, invoicing and so on.

For most businesses, this is where their brand begins and ends. Day after day we see brochures, websites and flyers proudly displaying endless pages of feature-driven copy, announcing mind-numbing technical details boasting how the Mark III widget is 'unique' because of its ninge-wheel boggit spring – something, according to the company's claims, that its competitors' products don't have.

Let's take the case of a slogan used for M&Ms (a Mars product) in the United States, which was also used for milk chocolate Treets in the United Kingdom for many years: 'Melts in your mouth, not in your hands.' To many feature-led marketers, the emphasis would be on the product's crisp candy shell – the covering that actually prevents the chocolate from leaking out. But in isolation, that's just a feature, and a pretty unimportant one to me. That's why features alone are not enough.

... and benefits

When features by themselves no longer appeared to generate sales, the focus shifted to benefits. In the 1960s, Rosser Reevers, chair of the New York advertising agency Ted Bates & Co, developed the idea of a *unique selling proposition* (sometimes called *unique selling point*). In his book *Reality in Advertising* (1961), Reeves laid down three rules about a USP:

- The proposition to the customer should be 'Buy this product, and you will get this specific benefit.'
- The proposition itself must be unique.
- The proposition must be strong enough to pull new customers to the product.

For several decades, the idea of the USP drove the sales and marketing strategies of companies large and small. Other models followed in the same path, emphasising the benefit of the product or service over just its physical attributes and capabilities.

This emphasis on the benefit that would be gained by those features was a significant step forward at the time for marketing. David Ogilvy, the grand-master of advertising, often recited a little ditty to emphasise this approach:

Tell me this, and tell me true
Or else, my friend, to hell with you

Less how your product came to be
And more of what it will do for me.

The problem is, this type of benefit is only half the story, and one that isn't sufficiently powerful on its own in the 21st century. The type of benefit promised by the USP is essentially a *tangible benefit* – something that is directly related to the product or service feature. For example, in the past, marketers would often explain that 'people don't buy drill bits, they buy a device to make a hole in the wall'. The hole in the wall was perceived as the main (and usually the only) benefit.

However, this is a limited view of a benefit for today's customer, because it implies that the benefit is purely in a *material* form – that is, the hole in the wall. Some marketing professionals would argue that it isn't even a benefit, merely an advantage! But semantics to one side, benefits today must go beyond a product or service's basic functions into the realms of *emotion*. In other words, the hole in the wall has a purpose beyond just being a hole! Perhaps it is to hang a picture there (see Figure 2.2), a painting that gives emotional pleasure to the viewer; maybe it's a certificate that evokes

FEATURE   **TANGIBLE BENEFIT**   **EMOTIONAL BENEFIT**

Figure 2.2   Feature, tangible benefit and emotional benefit

emotions of pride and satisfaction in having attained some qualification. It might even be to fix an ornament, a trophy, a family heirloom... something that draws an emotive benefit each time it is viewed. The USP of yesteryear has become the ESP (Emotional Selling Point) of today.

Maslow's Hierarchy of Human Needs

Why has the emphasis shifted so much towards creating emotional benefits for today's customers? In 1943 the psychologist Abraham Maslow proposed a theory for human motivation and established what he called his 'Hierarchy of Human Needs'. Maslow believed that, as humans, we seek to satisfy successively 'higher' needs that occupy a set hierarchy, and used a pyramid (see Figure 2.3) to show how these needs are prioritised into five different levels:

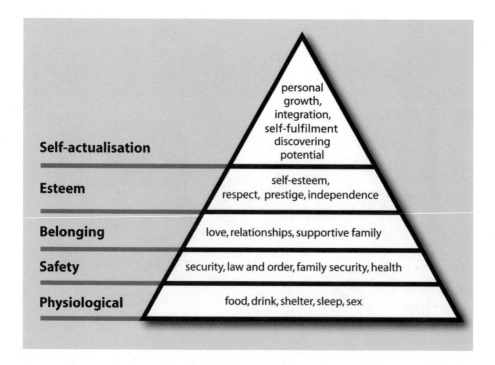

Figure 2.3   Feature, tangible benefit and emotional benefit

- *physiological needs*: basics such as food, drink, shelter, sleep and sexual activity;
- *safety needs*: physical security, security of employment, security of revenues and resources, law and order (security of personal property against crime), family security and health security;
- *belongingness, love and social needs*: the need for love and affection, relationships, a supportive and communicative family, belongingness to a group and sexual intimacy;
- *esteem needs*: the need for self-esteem, self-respect, self-mastery and independence, plus dominance, prestige, and the need for both respect and esteem from others;
- *self-actualisation needs*: the desire for personal growth, integration, and finding self-fulfilment through realising one's potential. Maslow states that this was a continual drive that could never be wholly fulfilled; rather, each achievement would simply motivate the individual to reach for even higher goals.

How does Maslow's Hierarchy of Human Needs relate to branding your business today? Well, most people (certainly most of your existing and prospective customers), have already met their needs at the lower levels of the pyramid. The so-called higher needs are therefore going to become much more a focus of their thoughts.

In fact, I'd like to propose my own theory here: I contend that when it comes to the lower levels of Maslow's hierarchy, then we're talking about the plain old *features and benefits* model. After all, if you just want a drink, you don't need a Starbucks Grande. Maybe you'll settle for tap water. You're satisfying a need. And the benefit is strictly physical: you get to quench your thirst. That's all, nothing else. But when you aspire to those higher levels, you move into an emotional arena. You've satisfied those tangible benefits, so now you want something more. You want to feel something, be someone, get somewhere. Feeling good about yourself, having status and recognition, and fulfilling your desires... now we're talking emotions. And if that's where society is focused right now, then your business ought to acknowledge that by building a brand through the power of emotion.

Consider, for instance, the need to connect with others. As we'll see in the chapter on storytelling, our society has become fragmented and has lost its tribal or group membership roots as technology has replaced dialogue. Yet humans have an innate need to be a part of something, to have ongoing dialogue and communication. That's why we've seen the rapid growth of blogs, wikis, chatrooms and social networks like Facebook and MySpace that attempt to bring people together so that they can bond and form relationships. Even McDonald's and Starbucks have become places where people gather together to talk. They are as much a social gathering as a refuelling station. *Does your product or service fulfil any needs at this level?*

What about esteem needs? People want to feel important, have respect and be made to feel special. Does your product or service do that... and if not, what would you need to change to make it happen? Then there are issues of trust and reliability. *Does your product or service build trust?* Is it something that customers rely on? If so, how can you express these things emotionally? And last, but by no means least, how can your product or service help people to self-actualise and develop themselves? Does it help them, assist them and support them? *Does your product or service enrich their lives and perhaps the lives of those around them, too, such as family and friends?* Again, how can you express this in an emotional way?

Remember, it's the product/service features, tangible benefits and emotional benefit of the product or service along with the *total experience* of dealing with your business that keeps your brand in the mind of the customer. A lot of marketing 'gurus' throw the baby out with the bathwater and focus attention only on the emotional side of the product. It's cute to promote the message that 'all you need is love'. But that's not how it works. So let me emphasise again: you need to communicate to your customers all three aspects: features, tangible benefits and emotional benefits. We could even emulate Maslow by creating a features and benefits hierarchy as shown in Figure 2.4.

As with Maslow's Hierarchy of Needs, the levels show how, when one aspect of the product or service is satisfied, the customer moves to the next level. It's still true, however, that no level exists in isolation. All three are important, and all three work together to give you a powerful product or service offering.

Adaptive or supportive emotions – you decide

It's all well and good to theorise about the need to develop emotional benefits for a product or service, but how can this be achieved in practice? To answer this, let's begin by defining the two kinds of emotional benefit that can be created for any product or service, including a non-profit.

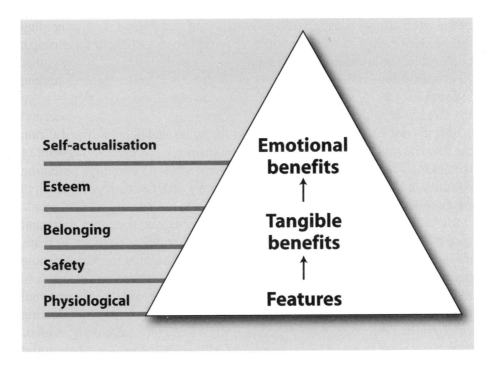

Figure 2.4   Features and benefits hierarchy

The first is what I call an *adaptive* approach. This is where the features and tangible benefits provide the platform on which to create an emotional benefit. For example, Volvo cars are built for safety. So, features might be the steel safety cage aspect of the car, or shock-absorbing zones, and tangible benefits could therefore be built around tangible aspects of passenger protection. But this could be taken much further when adapted as an emotional benefit. What about feelings of pride for choosing a car more for the safety of passengers than your own passion for, say, a sports car? A Volvo owner can comfortably state, 'I feel good as a purchaser of a Volvo, because it makes me a responsible, good person.' It certainly fulfils Maslow's criteria for respect, both from self and from others (who may be in admiration of the decision to put, say, family before self).

How about if you run a dental practice? You might have some of the latest X-ray machinery, which has features such as microprocessor technology and super-accurate imaging, which means that the dental treatment is enhanced. Again, you could use the description of the features and tangible benefits to create an emotional benefit based on an aspect of self-esteem, such as helping the client to have a movie-star smile, or to feel confident about their mouth and teeth when interacting with others.

In both examples the emotional benefit is directly linked to the features and rational benefits. You could say it's simply an emotional extension to what has already been described in physical terms.

But it's not always necessary to build the emotional benefit directly from the features and tangible benefits. We could simply use these as supporting details for a separate emotional benefit. Remember, no one buys purely on emotion or on logic. Purchases are emotionally led, but there still needs to be some rationality involved in the process.

Here's an example of a *supportive* approach. Let's imagine you're a paint manufacturer. You have a number of features regarding your paint. Perhaps there are certain features of the pigment that make the paint thicker, meaning that fewer applications are needed. The paint could also contain a special ingredient that makes it odour-free. These features could be turned into rational benefits such as faster completion of decorating, and in a comfortable environment. But none of these points really extend into emotional benefits. In that case, we need to look at some of Maslow's higher need levels and find out what emotion we could use to drive our paint brand. How about confidence in the ability to create a stunning décor by using this brand of paint? Or the pride one can feel when showing off one's achievement to friends and work colleagues?

In this scenario, the features and tangible benefits don't drive the emotional benefit; it's a stand-alone aspect of the brand, created separately (and deliberately) to introduce an emotion into the mix. But remember, people buy on emotion and justify with logic. So the emotional benefit drives the purchase, but it's supported by all the rational and tangible features and benefits.

Is either approach better than the other? I don't believe so. It's really just a question of what's appropriate. Sometimes, when the features and rational benefits are very strong, the emotional benefit is easy to create. At other times, features and benefits don't immediately produce an emotional state, so one has to be created. The important point is that all three elements are utilised. OK, now it's your turn. See how well you can create your own emotional benefit. I've provided another example of *adaptive* and *supportive* approaches to help you get to grips with what we're trying to achieve.

Defining your product or service's emotional benefit

The process of defining your product or service's emotional benefit should be done as a worksheet exercise.

1. List the features (eg size, weight, shape, colour, ingredients, specifications) of your product/service.
2. Then, describe what those features give the customer in terms of *tangible* benefits (ie physical, observable advantages of using the product or service). The best way to do this is to use the phrase 'which means that' after each feature and then add a statement detailing what practical benefit that feature will provide. Let's imagine we run a small business manufacturing or retailing sunglasses. Table 2.1 shows an example of possible features and tangible benefits.

Table 2.1   Features and tangible benefits of AcmeXYZ sunglasses

Feature	which means that	Benefit
Extra-powerful photochromatic lenses		You have better protection for your eyes.
Sturdy construction		They won't break if you accidentally drop them.
Lightweight frame		You won't find them uncomfortable to wear.

Now think through all those tangible benefits and find one emotional benefit that could satisfy customer needs at one of Maslow's higher levels: esteem, connection and belonging, confidence, achievement, etc. The emotion doesn't have to be an extension of the product's tangible benefits, although it could if the tangible benefits offered an emotional benefit by default.

Stuck for some emotional descriptions? Choose an emotion from the following list of emotional words, but make sure the emotion is *relevant* to the tangible benefits of your product or service. And don't try to muddy the waters by introducing lots of different emotional benefits. One is all you need to build the emotional pull of your product or service.

Feelings your product or service could evoke:

affection	amusement	amazement
bliss	caring	cheer
competence	confidence	contentment
coolness	cordiality	curiosity
devotion	eagerness	earnest
elation	empathy	enjoyment
enthusiasm	envy	excitement
expectancy	faithfulness	fascination
friendliness	frivolity	fun
generosity	gentleness	gratefulness
happiness	hope	humour
inspiration	interest	joy
light-heartedness	loving	optimism
passion	peace	pleasure
pride	relief	resilience
respect	rest	romance
sadness	satisfaction	sensitivity
serenity	sincerity	stimulation
surprise	sympathy	

In our example above, the benefits centre around safety, durability and comfort. We could focus our emotional benefit on trust, for example. We could emphasise the fact that AcmeXYZ sunglasses won't let you down when they're needed. Then we could communicate that emotional message by selecting lifestyle examples of people undertaking risky or daring adventures where reliability of the glasses was paramount. If relevant, we could even involve humour (though it must be treated with care). If you've understood the previous explanation, you'll recognise that the features and tangible benefits here are *adaptives*; we've adapted them to fit an emotional benefit.

Let's take an example of male sunglasses. Imagine Horatio Caine in *CSI Miami* reaching for his trademark sunglasses as he prepares to deliver one of his cool one-liners, only to watch them fall to bits on the ground. The director shouts, 'Cut.' The scene becomes chaotic. Studio hands attempt to repair the shades, but to no avail. Horatio turns to face the camera and says, 'Better get AcmeXYZ sunglasses before the next episode!' Would you remember that? Would it make you laugh? Could it create an emotion in you that suggested AcmeXYZ sunglasses could be trusted more than other brands?

But wait a moment; aren't we getting carried away here? If you're a smallish business that just happens to make or sell eyewear, you might be thinking, 'How could I afford to pay someone like David Caruso to endorse my product?' The answer is that you don't need to. You just need to be a little creative. Why not do a spoof of Caine using some low-cost actors, or even offer someone from the local drama school an opportunity to feature in a promotional campaign? Why not hold a David Caruso lookalike competition, the winner to feature in your marketing material? That alone will generate publicity guaranteed to raise the awareness of your company and its product.

With a little brainstorming, you could have the makings of a great emotional platform on which to build your brand. You could feature the entire parody as part of your public relations, advertising and publicity materials. You could demonstrate the sunglasses in shopping malls and inside stores, using the Horatio lookalike or spoof character as part of the pitch. Again, this will generate spin-off activity such as newspapers and radio stations picking up on the whole theme. As I said earlier, the emotion does not need to be tied to the features and tangible benefits as in the adaptive approach. It could be something entirely separate.

Remember (and forgive me for continually driving this home), customers purchase goods and services on the basis of emotion, but use logic as their justification. I might purchase a new PC from Dell because I am emotionally tied to that particular brand. However, I'm still impressed by the features and tangible benefits of dual-core processing technology, huge amounts of memory and mega-big hard drives. In this regard, the emotion I feel for the brand may not be based upon the technological benefits. After all, as an average consumer, I may not even understand them.

Supporting your emotional benefit

So let's look at another scenario involving the *supportive* approach. We've already seen some features and tangible benefits of the sunglasses. But what about style? How would wearing them make me feel? What emotions would stir inside of me as I donned those shades? As a male, would I suddenly become Horatio Caine in my mind's eye? If I'm a female, which role model, mentor or favourite celebrity do I become? Am I suddenly a star in *Sex in the City* or am I the all-powerful Miranda from *The Devil Wears Prada*? Power, self-esteem, respect... perhaps even snobbery. None of these emotions are adaptations of the features and rational benefits. But it doesn't matter. You wouldn't even be considering purchasing the sunglasses in the first place if you didn't feel comfortable about the rational attributes.

How do you know whether to use an *adaptive* approach or a *supportive* approach? The answer is, it depends on the product or service you're offering. Products and services that deal directly with self-worth (cosmetics and grooming, healthcare and fitness, holidays and leisure activities, etc) lend themselves to developing great emotional themes without the need for careful scrutiny of the rational and tangible aspects, so only *supportives* are needed. Not-for-profits will also generally be dealing with a highly emotive subject by default, so s*upportives* can be used simply to enhance and provide the rationale for making the purchase or giving a donation. For instance, a charity dealing with the plight of homeless people can raise emotions of empathy, anger at injustice, or sorrow at their predicament. This, in turn, can create an emotional benefit for the donor such that by giving to the charity, they can feel good about themselves and their concern for their fellow human beings.

On the other hand, supplying bags of cement, selling industrial coatings or operating a PC repair business may not provide the same level of opportunity to create a powerful 'stand-alone' emotional benefit, in which case opt for the *adaptive* approach.

I once presented a seminar on branding where a marketing manager attendee from a small wire-making business asked how to create an emotional benefit for a set of bicycle wheel spokes. Her frustrations stemmed from what she thought was a really boring product (with little to show even in rational benefit terms). In addition, her products were sold to bicycle manufacturers who then sold on to the end user, so she felt confused about just who ought to be getting the emotional benefit anyway – assuming one could eventually be unearthed. How would you have created (or discovered) an emotional benefit in this seemingly difficult situation?

I looked at some of the product's features (which were the only thing mentioned on the technical data sheet that was about all the company had by way of promotional literature). I knew very little about bicycle spokes, but learned that there were specific gauges of wire that produced optimum results. I learned that the spokes are vital components that have to be carefully manufactured because they are under constant tension, so the wire was thicker near the threads, where the stress would be at its highest. These features alone can easily provide tangible benefits of safety and security. Would a bicycle manufacturer be concerned about issues of safety and reliability in the materials used in its own bicycle construction? Of course it would. What's more, anyone in the buying department wants to be reassured that the company is purchasing the best. And while quality assurance marks of one kind or another are a rational way to show a product's quality level, it takes the generating of positive emotions to help buyers feel they are making wise purchasing decisions and be confident about a product's dependability.

In the end, the spoke supplier created an emotional benefit of trust, using the features and rational benefits as adaptives. One particular promotional campaign featured a close-up of a bicycle wheel, showing the spokes, with a headline that said, 'These are the spokes that hold the hubs that turn the wheels that steer your bikes that take your customers on a never-ending adventure.' The copy went on to cover all the features and tangible benefits of the spokes, then linked these emotionally to the trust the cycle manufacturer could have in the wire-maker's product. It could have stopped there, but so impressed was one cycle manufacturer that its marketing department utilised the same theme as part of its own brand campaign, changing it to a supportive approach by creating the separate emotional benefit of freedom. All the product features and tangible benefits became supportives for a powerful campaign involving close-up shots of various parts of the bicycle in different settings: a city, a country road, a mountain scene – wherever and whenever the cyclists wanted to go to 'get away from it all'.

The result? Not only did this enhance the wire-maker's brand but the relationship with that particular cycle manufacturer was deepened – so much so that the cycle manufacturer signed an exclusive five-year contract with the spoke company.

So far, we've covered the importance of generating an emotional benefit for your product or service. But, as hopefully you know by now, that's only part of the story. A brand, remember, is the *total experience* a customer has of your company – not just what it sells. This means that all the customer service surrounding the pre-purchase, purchase and post-purchase activity must carry an emotional benefit that both supports and enhances the emotions you've generated for your product or service.

Does the United Kingdom lead the way for appalling customer service? The British Market Research Bureau conducted a survey on behalf of the Abbey National bank. The results revealed that workers in Britain spend a total of 56 million days a year waiting at home for deliveries or repairmen only to have many of those days wasted because as many as 4 out of 10 workmen never arrive, while others turn up late. The worst record for late arrivals, according to the survey, was for electrical goods deliveries, with furniture arrivals in a close second place.

That said, customers don't necessarily want to experience emotions pertaining to freedom, adventure, personal health, intimacy and grooming, etc as part of your customer service, even though those emotions may surround the product or service itself. Status and social recognition generally don't play a part either.

When other branding books suggest that the customer experience should be 'seamless in its emotional offerings', I don't disagree. You do, however, need to be aware of emotional benefit conflicts. Let me illustrate with an example. Virgin has a particular approach to its brand that includes a somewhat irreverent style of humour, often being quite disrespectful to the more pompous British establishment – a brand strategy that has so far done well for the Virgin empire, and is consistent with Sir Richard's own 'rebellious' nature. So, when using its various products and services, you'd probably expect to encounter aspects of fun and frolics, be it on the airline or watching one of Virgin's risqué viral marketing campaigns. But that doesn't mean that when you telephone Virgin's head office you are treated in a disrespectful way, or that Virgin staff have a laugh at your expense. Like all powerful brands, Virgin takes its brand seriously and knows when and where to draw the line.

On the other hand, a funeral service that offers an emotional benefit of empathy, or trust, would need to ensure that this emotion was key to the customer experience in all aspects of its brand. When you are running a business, my advice would be that the brand experience should ensure that the customer feels:

- respected;
- appreciated;
- valued;
- listened to;
- safe buying from you;
- good about choosing your company;
- confident about trusting you;
- connected to your company;
- that you care about others, the environment and society.

When you have achieved all of the above, you can then work towards your customers having:

- feelings of positive anticipation for the next time they deal with you;
- feelings of passion about your company and what it stands for;

and even:

- feelings of infatuation with your company (if you reach this level, you should write the next book on branding).

Where the emotional benefits of the product or service are the same, then integrate them into your brand experience, as much as you can. But if there's any kind of clash or potential confusion, keep them well apart.

Most books on branding will state that customer experiences should be a reflection of your brand values. That's true enough. As you'll see in the chapter on creating your Brand Storybook™ (Chapter 16), communicating your philosophy about your business, why you started it and where you want it to go is a powerful way to win the hearts of your desired audience. But I also believe that the customer experience should mirror the customer's values, too. In fact, your customer base should be built around those people whose values are linked to yours. The key point here, albeit a semantic one, is that focusing on the customer's values rather than simply your own becomes an outside-in dynamic, rather than an inside-out static mentality. In other words, previous marketing models depended on a business finding a customer and then offering the goods and services the business wanted that customer to buy. It didn't really matter about any kind of emotional connection, just as long as the customer was satisfied with the purchase and the service that surrounded it.

In today's world of increasingly comparable products, similar service levels and very few physical differentiators, the inside-looking-out approach will no longer secure the long-term loyalty of a customer. But find someone who likes you, because they are to one degree or another like you, and you'll have a much better chance of building a powerful and sustainable brand.

As Dr E Doyle McCarthy (1989) put it, 'Emotion is a fundamental social category, a mould for our mental lives. Emotions themselves are objects we handle and seek in that contemporary drama of the self.'

Yes, emotions are internal figures that play out their lives in the theatre of the body. We are creatures of emotion. Businesses need to understand that – more than at any other time in history – the way to a customer's wallet or purse is not just via the head but must include – and indeed focus on – the heart. Now that we have learned just how important emotions are, we need to understand how we actually trigger them in our customer experience.

3

Perception is reality

Reality is merely an illusion, albeit a very persistent one.

Albert Einstein

How perception creates emotion

So far, we've seen that emotion is at the heart and core of a powerful brand. But what has to happen, and how, for emotions to be invoked in customers?

In the past decade or so, a greater emphasis has been placed on what has become known as 'customer care'. The early days of this approach were quite basic, and often involved rote learning of scripts used by front-line staff who were less than engaged with the brand, let alone the customer. Gimmicks, rather than true customer-focused strategies, were often the order of the day. In particular, the sentiment of 'have a nice day' displayed on badges worn by staff (see Figure 3.1) was often not matched by employee attitudes, a lot of the time because they were not aligned to the values and ideals of the business for which they worked. What's more, while 'nice day' greetings met with some success in the more service-oriented culture of the United States, they were scorned and derided by staff and customers alike throughout the United Kingdom, who saw the badges as nothing more than plain sarcasm.

The biggest problem with customer care, however, was not with its intentions. The motive of attempting to provide more of what the customer wanted was good. Where it was flawed was in the assumption that customer care meant 'being nice' to the customer, which in turn would lead to greater levels of consumer loyalty and repeat purchasing.

The trouble is, customers don't think like that – especially in today's abundance-of-choice marketplace, where 'being nice' is a given. That's why although customer care sentiments of being kind and polite are important, they are only part of a much bigger overall brand experience that needs to be created in order to evoke a powerful consumer emotion.

Figure 3.1 'Have-a-nice-day' badges (derided in the United Kingdom)

But how are these emotions generated? We've already discovered that previous marketing models limited to logic and rationality are outdated, although they do have a place in defining the brand. After all, the product or service has to be affordable to those at whom it is aimed. And, of course, it also has to deliver 'what it says on the tin'. But once these essentials are taken care of, the only thing left is the emotions. When consumers buy a BMW or Mercedes, they want to be certain that there are still four wheels on it, an engine, seating and so on. But any car can supply these features. Not every car can supply the emotions that go with them, however. As any Harley-Davidson motorbike owner will testify, a Harley is more than a bike; it represents a free spirit, independence and adventure – all emotive, none of which you'll find in features alone.

Generating emotions

What, then, creates emotions? Where do they come from?

They are generated as the result of *perception*. Aaron T Beck, one of the founding fathers of the popular cognitive behavioural therapy, said, 'emotion follows perception'. As we'll discover, the reverse is also true, in that perception can be shaped by emotion; like many aspects of the brain's information-processing routine, it's a two-way street.

Our first objective was to create an emotional benefit for our customers. That benefit needs to be experienced for it to have any effect. So, in order to evoke emotion, we first need to trigger it through perception.

What is perception?

'Perception' comes from the Latin word *percipere*, which means *to seize* or *to understand*. Perception is the process by which the brain organises and interprets information brought in through the senses or created in our imagination, combined with stored information in memory, enabling us to construct an understanding of the world around us.

Notice that I used the word 'construct'. You've probably heard the saying 'Perception is reality', and in this context it's true. Our understanding of the world is not the world itself but a construction in our mind that fits a number of criteria, much of which is personal to us. When a customer deals with your business, he or she will arrive at a perception of the customer experience you have provided. If it's not the way you wanted that customer to perceive your business, that's tough – and you've got work to do (which is why you bought this book).

But the point I'm making here is that, once again, the customer owns the brand experience, not you. The customer determines the 'reality' of the experience, not you. And the customer votes to support that reality by remaining a loyal supporter of your brand – or hightail it out of town to look for other, better 'realities' to experience.

To demonstrate what I mean about the customer's 'reality', take a look at the following picture (Figure 3.2). What do you see?

Many of you will immediately notice that it's a picture of a young woman, complete with necklace and a feather in her hair. 'That's not what I see,' other readers might exclaim. 'I see a three-quarter view of an old woman with a huge nose and a chin buried in her coat.'

Whenever I show this picture as part of a presentation on branding and ask the audience who sees what, the room is often split 50–50 as to who sees the young woman and who sees the old. Even more interesting is that many in the audience can only see one or the other, even when they've been told about the alternative view. The point is, what you saw was *your* perception – which may have been different from someone else's.

Figure 3.2 Alternative 'realities'

Your understanding of what the picture represented was created (or perceived if you will) inside your mind. In fact, because the picture is ambiguous – it could be either a young woman or an old woman – the perception has relied upon your drawing on your own mental storehouse of shapes and features to determine for yourself what you are observing. Even before we get into a deeper understanding about perception, this raises a vital point about delivering a powerful brand experience:

> The more ambiguous your customer experience, the less likely your brand will be perceived correctly.

In other words, if I wanted to make sure you saw only the young woman, what would I have to change in the picture? Perhaps not very much, just a

Figure 3.3   Focusing people's perceptions

few lines here and there to limit the ability to see anything but her face. In fact, let's do just that. For those of you who couldn't see the young woman before, does this illustration help (Figure 3.3)?

I've amended and altered certain bits of the illustration to limit the perception to the young woman. The old woman's nose and chin are no longer prominent in the picture. And so it is with your total customer experience. It must be designed as you want it to be. If not, the customer will draw heavily upon internal resources to try to make sense of your brand, rather than be helped by clear, consistent messages and experiences.

In order to understand the process of perception, let's state a simple formula that sums up what perception is all about:

Sensation + Information = Perception

Perception, then, is not the same thing as sensation. Sensation is a physical (or physiological) process and has to do with obtaining information about the world around us via our senses. In the case of the picture shown in Figure 3.3, it was lines and shapes that created specific sensations. But sensations do not merely pass through the brain and come out the other side as a perception. How did you know that those lines represented the shape of a face? How did you know what a face was in the first place? Sensory information alone was simply not enough, so your brain processed additional information and helped you form conclusions about what those senses had identified. It is this whole process that we call perception.

Rather than get bogged down in lots of psychological models to show how perception works, let's look at the process in simple terms – and where we can influence the customer the most. The flow diagram shown in Figure 3.4

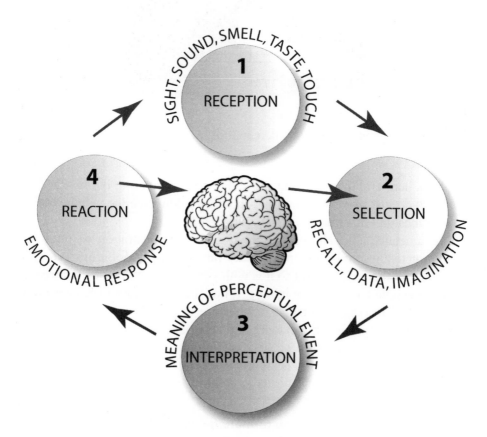

Figure 3.4   The four major parts of perception

is a general explanation of what takes place in the act of perception, from the initial input of sensory information through to the storage of information in long-term memory. (As I've already mentioned, long-term memory is where brands reside, so this is a key component in building our emotional customer experience.)

One caveat. In constructing a diagram like this, it's important that we don't fall into the trap of the previous marketing models we discussed and view the workings of the brain as a simple linear device, or a series of connected 'black boxes' with just an input and output. Many different parts of the brain are operating simultaneously, sometimes influencing single parts of the operation but very often having involvement in the whole process. Pathways are not flowing merely in two directions, but in many different directions at once.

Looking at our perception diagram, we can see that there are essentially four major parts to its operation:

Reception → Selection → Interpretation → Reaction

In the following chapters we'll look at each aspect of this perception diagram in turn.

Perception and long-term memory

RECEPTION

Figure 4.1 Reception of experiences of the world through the senses

Our experience of the physical and material world around us (and therefore our customer experience) is first received through our senses. Traditionally, it has been assumed that there are just five senses: sight, sound, smell, taste and touch. Today, we understand that there are many more senses, including those of motion, heat, balance and bodily awareness, although some scientists argue that these are merely subsets of the standard five. For the purpose of creating our emotional generators we'll stay with the traditional set, because they are the main triggers that businesses can use for evoking emotions.

In customers who have all their senses in working order, these five senses will provide the way in which the physical world is transmitted to the brain:

- *Sight:* the eyes respond to light.
- *Sound:* the ear responds to sound waves.
- *Smell:* the nose contains olfactory receptors that distinguish smells.
- *Taste:* the tongue's taste receptors identify different tastes.
- *Touch:* receptors all over the body respond to touch.

It's possible for all of these senses to work separately, but most of the time they work together, either as a combination to create another sensation or as coordinators to keep what we experience 'in sync'. For instance, smell and taste can work together to create flavour: the smell of a particular cheese coupled with its taste will supply its unique flavour. Neither sense on its own can do this. If the cheese is mouldy or has some other visual aspect to it that looks unpleasant, this visual input can easily override any aspects of flavour or taste, changing your response from one of delight to one of disgust.

Equally important is coordination of the senses. When we listen to someone speak, we may only be concerned with the sense of sound. But when we are engaged in a conversation with someone, we are processing visual information, too. In this regard, speech and sight need to be well coordinated. Imagine if every time someone spoke, their mouths appeared to move out of synchronisation with the words you were hearing (rather like some of those very poorly overdubbed movies and commercials you often see).

What's more, information arriving at one or two senses may evoke other sensations as part of the perception process, simply because they are linked together in your mind. Watching your favourite food being prepared and experiencing its smell at the same time may make your mouth water, much like Pavlov's dog salivating at the sound of a bell that signalled feeding time. Listening to someone laugh may cause you to smile, even though you might not know what the laughter is all about. Both of these scenarios can also fire the imagination, or you might recall a past experience as a result of those senses. The sight and smell of delicious food, besides causing you to salivate, may also bring to mind vivid memories of occasions where you enjoyed such food with a loved one, or group of friends. And even if you don't know what caused the stranger to laugh, the event might cause you to remember a time when you, too, had a really good laugh about something. Such responses are all part of the brain's association and recall activity, as we shall soon discover.

Even more important for us, we can discover how each of these aspects of perception can be influenced to the advantage of the customer's positive brand experience.

SELECTION

Figure 4.2   Selection of sensory experience

With (at least) five senses in operation, the amount of information being fed into our brain is colossal. We may see over 10,000 brand communication messages every day, coming at us from posters, websites, radio, television and word of mouth. We are constantly bombarded with different colours, themes, sounds and shapes all relating to different brands.

How does this huge pile of information flowing through our senses get processed by the brain's limited capacity? It doesn't. Once the data from our sensory receptors hit the area of the brain we call sensory memory, an intricate filtering process begins, much of it (probably 95 per cent) entirely without our conscious awareness. It is here, a part of the selection point in our diagram, that sensory information is stored – often for just a fraction of a second – after the actual sensation has ended.

By the time information coming via our senses leaves the sensory memory area of the brain, it is already a much smaller set of data. It then passes to the second stage of the selection process, known as working memory. At this stage, information held in various memory circuits of the brain relating to similar previous sensory experiences, along with other types of information stored in our brain about our beliefs, values, etc, is combined with the here-and-now influences. In fact, there are a number of criteria that must be considered in order for the brain to select the 'best picture' of the current sensory experience and decide how to respond to the situation. Figure 4.3 shows a typical list of filters that will have an effect on how we perceive what's happening. Notice from the illustration how these filters are subjective. Few of these existed when we were born – at least, not in a way that could make much sense at the

Figure 4.3   Influences on our perception

time. Our memories – the brain's warehouse of everything from the smallest piece of information to the most vivid experiences – have developed over our lifetime, with the brain continually adding new items to its storage space.

No two people will filter the same experiences in the same way or hold identical beliefs about everything. Even basic likes and dislikes, such as the kind of music you listen to, what political party you support, or the choice of your favourite football team, will be built around your personal belief system. It's unlikely that any of these preferences will be derived from hard facts. Most will be assembled from personal experiences, biases and assumptions, however inaccurate they may be.

For example, does everyone go shopping for designer-label clothes? Many do, enough to create a worldwide market. These consumers have a belief system that allows designer gear a 'natural' place in their filters. But for others, designer labels are symbols of excess and find no place in their value system. They might deem themselves 'nonconformist' by boycotting anything except, perhaps, street clothing. However, as the number of street clothing wearers increases, the nonconformists become conformists in their own social group. (Don't you just love the way the human mind works?)

One study of urban low-income consumers in Bolivia by Luuk van Kempen (2004) showed that, as a group, they were willing to pay a premium for the designer label as a symbol. This depended on the group's relative economic situation, education level and the frequency with which they watched soaps on television.

What we know from research is that even if people are shown that a particular belief held in their memory is incorrect, they'll adapt any conflicting information to 'make it fit' the belief they hold. That's often a reason why brands fail to make an impact on their customers: they simply don't share the same common beliefs, or they attempt to change a long-held belief that is deeply set in the customer's memory bank simply by supplying cold facts – the smallest component of perception!

Of course, it's impossible to match every single belief a person holds. But the closer you get to really understanding the way your customers think about the particular kind of product or service you sell, and the way in which it is offered, the more likely you are to create the kind of influence on their perception that will generate the right kind of emotional response.

Understanding the scheme of things

How in the world can we influence perception when there appear to be so many fragmented pieces of information in the customer's head? Well, fortunately, information is thought to be stored in our memory in the form of what psychologists call *schemata*: clusters of information about particular items or issues. For instance, one cluster (schema) might link information together that is to do with ourselves, such as who we are, the role we play as, say, a parent, or employee, or the type of personality that we portray. Another schema might be a cluster of information about the social group we belong to, our position in it and the stereotypes we may have created, while another might connect knowledge about events or circumstances.

Even if the customer is expected to draw upon his or her imagination, the images, sounds and feelings conveyed 'in the mind' will need to reference events already experienced. Imagination is always viewed through the beliefs, biases and prejudices that you hold. Without them, imagination has severe limitations. If you've never been in a helicopter, trying to imagine what it would be like could prove quite difficult. You might access previous experiences of flying, or being at the top of a high building, but nothing suitable will be present in memory to help create accurate ideas about something not yet experienced. So what happens? The mind simply takes a 'best guess' – which often turns out to be wildly off the mark. Imagination simply can't make new jumps in belief with no prior experience to reference.

This is yet another important consideration in creating a powerful brand through our total customer experience. All too often, companies and not-for-profits use publicity or fundraising campaigns that rely heavily on the customer (or donor) using imagination as the key driver to purchase the product, or support the cause. An example is the countless number of fundraising mailers I've received over the years that ask me to 'imagine what it's like to go hungry for weeks at a time' or 'imagine what it's like to be told you have a terminal illness'.

Fortunately, neither of these undesirable things has happened to me… but the point is, I can't imagine them! How can I? As I've never been in either situation (for which I'm eternally grateful), the sender is asking me to construct a schema for which I have no reference. Oh, sure, I can think about times when I've been hungry, and I can think about occasions when I've been ill. But they are inadequate sources of information for my perceptual processing. It's unlikely that either headline will evoke an emotional response that's intense enough for me to support the worthy cause. And you know what? It never has.

We'll see shortly how this directly relates to the intensity and consistency of our customer's brand experience. But before we get there, here's an exercise for you:

Can you think of ways in which your customer experience can perpetuate and intensify the relevant schemata – and even create new ones?

INTERPRETATION

Figure 4.4 Interpretation of sensory experience

Now that the brain has gathered together the information it needs in order to prepare a response to the current sensory experience, it needs to decide how to interpret the information in the most appropriate way. In severe circumstances of danger, for example, available information may be in the form of stored images, symbols and emotions resulting from previous experiences relating to the danger being faced.

A decision will need to be made as to whether one should stay to fight or if the best option is that of flight. In other words, the memory store of schemata collected for a particular situation does not necessarily have an already determined result (we've already seen how the little almond-shaped device called the amygdala can be quick off the mark to make a hasty decision – one that could be way off base). So, the brain needs to connect this information with the information currently being received through the senses, then make a judgement call on what the best course of action by way of response is going to be.

This interpretation of events has an enormous bearing on our customer brand experience. Suppose that a customer had a really bad time with a member of staff at an electrical store – maybe one of your competitors. The customer had purchased an item that didn't perform correctly and brought it back for a replacement. An argument ensued. After heated exchanges, the customer felt badly treated and left, threatening to sue the company and to never do business with it again. A few months later, the same customer buys an item from your store and it too turns out to be faulty. Once again, she finds herself at the beginning of a situation already stored in memory.

Stop right now. What do you think her schema for that previous customer experience might be at this precise moment in time? Her perceptual system is evaluating the situation by drawing on that past experience, combining it with the various filters of belief, values, preferences and so on, and determining what appropriate response should be prepared in readiness for a possible ordeal. It could swing either way.

The interpretation of information could mean that the customer is now expecting to be treated badly and is already prepared to stay and 'fight' to get the right customer service. Before your salesperson can even enquire as to the problem, the customer is already on the defensive, emotions rising, moving swiftly into battle position. Alternatively, the customer might have a belief system that says, 'Don't make waves, don't cause trouble.' She might decide that submission is the better option, doesn't want to face another hostile encounter and therefore departs from the store, willing to accept a passive end to a negative situation that hasn't even occurred yet! And she never comes back.

You think this scenario is far-fetched? I've been in many situations in shops, restaurants and (my all-time favourite contentious spot) airports where, once a problem occurs, the observation of sensory processing is fascinating. Aggression, assertion, submission, frustration, depression... all the emotions are there (and not just from the customers!). All will have been generated by this amazing filter of stored memories, beliefs, ideals, values and the like.

Of course, you can't know what previous experiences your customers have got stored in their memory. You can't know in intricate detail all the perceptual filters that are being called into action in order to determine a response to a situation. But finding out some of the main preferences in this area and aligning your customer experience with them will greatly increase the chances of influencing perceptions.

REACTION

Figure 4.5   Reaction to sensory experience

When stored information is combined with the current data coming in from the senses, the brain decides on the most appropriate action. Neither the decision nor the result will be a conscious one. As we've seen, the reaction will depend on the types of schemata stored in memory and what they represent: positive or negative experiences, along with other stored influencers such as belief systems, values, ideals and so on, used by the brain to reach a decision on the type of response to be made. Remember, it is the interpretation of what's happening rather than the event itself that will cause a particular emotional response to occur. If there is no previous schema in the customer's memory from which to draw information, it's likely that there will be little or no emotional response.

At this stage, then, this decision is now ready to be played out by way of reaction. The response does not engage the use of the rational brain, but is entirely emotional in context and occurs in a matter of milliseconds. The reaction will not only include mental states but also take into account the mood of the customer at that particular time. It will also affect the senses that triggered the whole perceptual system in the first place. In many situations the reaction will not only trigger an emotion but also change the body's physical features such as facial gestures (we may display a wide smile, open our eyes wider, grimace or clench our teeth, depending on whether the situation is negative or positive). Our voice may change (we might lower or raise its intensity, or its pitch), our blood pressure rises, pulse and heart rate speed up or slow down, our sweat glands go into overdrive and even our digestive system reacts (say no more). Much of this will depend upon the intensity of the emotion, which will be determined by the nature of the situation we are focusing upon. Some psychologists pare this down to three main emotional identifiers:

- happy/unhappy;
- intense/mild;
- assertive/passive.

The myths of emotional branding

But beware! It is very easy to fall into the trap of generating any kind of emotional response, assuming that's all there is to it. Let's cover some emotional response myths right now.

- **Myth 1: The consumer will always remember the brand if they experience a deep emotional reaction.**
  Our total customer experience may include some aspects that arouse intense emotions – for example, an advertisement, brochure or commercial that depicts a scary scene, or causes a reaction of shock or disgust. Given that some emotional reactions can last a lifetime by being preserved in long-term memory, you might think that your customer experience strategy is going in the right direction. The thing to be careful of here, however, is that the intense emotion doesn't become the key focus rather than the brand behind it. So many advertising campaigns have featured emotional triggers, but although the viewer can recall the advertisement and perhaps even the smallest detail of the emotive content, they cannot recall the brand.

During the 1970s, an award-winning TV campaign in the United Kingdom for Cinzano featured comedy actor Leonard Rossiter and actor/author Joan Collins (probably best known internationally for her *Dynasty* role). The ads were created around Rossiter as a bungling fool always managing to accidentally throw his drink over the woman (Joan), oblivious to what he'd done. The ads were extremely funny and won several awards. The level of emotional intensity towards the ads was so strong that when the commercial channel ITV went on strike, viewers complained not about missing programmes but about missing the ads. The trouble was, while everyone liked and remembered the ads, research showed that not only did most viewers think the ads were for Martini – Cinzano's main rival – but Martini's sales actually went up.

- ■ **Myth 2: The more you get customers to use their imagination, the more intense the emotion will be.**
  We have already covered the fact that imagination needs reference to past experiences. The psychologist Nico Frijda (1988) stated that 'Emotions are elicited by events with meanings appraised as real, and their intensity corresponds to the degree to which this is the case.' Put simply, the closer the customer experience is to the customer's reality (remember, it's *their* reality, not yours!), the more likely the emotional reaction is. What's more, asking the customer to imagine some aspect of benefit, without a prior schema for reference, will undoubtedly bring about inaccurate expectations, to the detriment of the brand.
- ■ **Myth 3: The more emotions you generate at one time, the stronger the customer experience.**
  Humans can only experience one emotion at any given time. Granted, an emotion can be fleeting, and replaced quickly by another. Think of someone who has just checked what appears to be a winning lottery ticket... elation! On double-checking, however, two of the numbers were misread. Not a penny has been won. Emotional change? You bet (forgive the pun). But customer experiences work best when they are built around a consistent emotional theme. Not only does this avoid any conflicts of emotions along the way, but it is also a vital issue in creating your Brand Halo™.

■ **Myth 4: The best approach to a positive customer experience is to build emotional triggers around the belief that 'the customer is always right'.**

This one is based on another concept from the 1900s and perpetuated by the customer care movement of the 1990s. It was originally coined by Harry Gordon Selfridge, the American founder of the famous London retail store Selfridges. Once again, the whole social setting for purchasing products and services has moved on, but this old bromide is still offered up as a rational proposal in sales and marketing trainings all over the Western world.

But you know and I know that the customer is NOT always right, right? Customers may arrive at one of your customer experience points (we'll cover these Brand Reflections later) in a particular mood that doesn't match the customer experience that's been prepared. The idea that the Brand Halo™ should therefore be altered to accommodate a customer who is unjustifiably impatient, argumentative, aggressive or just plain misinformed is a bad strategy. It means, for example, that your employees – so vital in creating a powerful brand – have to put their own feelings and belief systems to one side and pretend to offer empathy or some other false emotion to the customer.

Sorry, but, despite what some branding experts say, a 'grin-and-bear-it' approach is not the way to build a brand. Of course, there is never any excuse to be impolite, disrespectful or cold towards a customer. But building a brand on the basis of pleasing customers from hell is a sure way to end up there. And anyway, you can't build a powerful brand on a lie. Mr Selfridge certainly didn't. He died penniless in 1947.

■ **Myth 5: Customer satisfaction surveys will show whether the emotional triggers are working.**

Sadly, no. Customer surveys are often the biggest red herring for a business seeking to improve its brand, simply because information fed back from the customer is taken at face value. The fact is, most customers when asked to rate satisfaction with a company's service will award it the highest mark, or the second highest. What companies usually fail to do is gather any information relating to the emotional commitment or loyalty to the brand – in other words, they gain feedback but not insight.

Many customers are loath to complain about anything, because they fear the whole brand relationship will be compromised. (Culture plays a part, too. People in the United Kingdom are much less likely to complain than their American or Canadian counterparts at, for instance, a poor restaurant experience; they just never go back. What's worse is that when the restaurant manager says, 'Was everything all right?' they often respond with a 'Yes, thank you, it was fine', as they head for the door.)

The best approach is to ascertain the most appropriate sensory influences using a brand perception survey rather than a typical customer satisfaction survey. There's one included later in this book.

LONG-TERM MEMORY

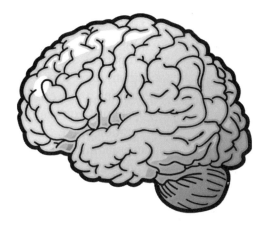

Figure 4.6   Long-term memory: the home of the brand

There is only one place in the entire universe that a brand resides. That's in the customer's *long-term memory*. Any other resting place in the mind is simply transient and it will fade very quickly, to be replaced by some other passing experience, probably destined for the same waste disposal chute that the thousands of rejected sensations, messages and stimulations disappear down every waking moment of life.

One thing that's good to know about long-term memory is that once our brand is resident in it, as long as it's maintained the chances are that it will stay there, unless some major experience alters the schema so much that there's a dramatic shift in content. As far as our customer experience goes, we need to focus on three key factors of pushing the brand into long-term memory:

1.   **The more intense the experience, the more likely it is to get to long-term memory, rather than being discarded on the way there.**
2.   **The more 'real' as opposed to abstract the experience, the more accessible this perceptual information will become.**
3.   **The more often the customer experience is visited by the customer, the higher the chances of it remaining in long-term memory.**

Of course, one important point about long-term memory is how we actually get the information back out, especially as it will be used as a reference against the brand experience currently happening. To do this, the brain uses what are known as 'retrieval cues'. These memory prompts basically act as reminders of the most appropriate information to utilise in the selection process, and they are usually embedded in memory along with the actual sensory experience that caused the memory in the first instance. However, further retrieval cues can create an important advantage in helping to recall brand information.

In fact, it is thought that lack of retrieval cues is one of the major causes of brand benefits being forgotten and therefore not helping to build the brand. In other words, it's not always that brand information gets lost in our long-term memories; once it arrives, it usually stays there. But if there are no ongoing retrieval cues, it's less likely that this information will be brought to the surface – ie to the conscious awareness – and utilised to support a purchasing decision.

That's why building a powerful brand is not just a one-off event. And that's why your Brand Halo™ is such a vital approach to consistently and continually influence your customers and supporters to keep your brand 'top of mind'.

In a 1987 study by Kevin Lane Keller, Assistant Professor of Marketing at Stanford University, consumers were shown advertisements for four different brands in four different product categories – cereal, laundry detergent, pain relievers and toothpaste – and were asked to evaluate each brand. Half of the respondents were then shown pack mock-ups that featured just the brand name of each product, while the other half were given mock-ups that not only included the brand name but a small version of the advertisement headline and picture too.

Consumers who viewed the pack mock-ups where only the brand name was displayed had low recall of the advertising product claims. But those who saw the mock-ups containing the brand name and advertisement extracts were able to remember specific product claims in the advertisement copy, even when the headline and picture used didn't relate directly to the advert copy that covered those claims. In addition, the inclusion of the advert headline and photo extracts prompted the respondents to give more favourable and in-depth evaluations of the brands.

The conclusions were that the advertising headline and photo on each of the pack mock-ups were acting as retrieval cues, allowing the consumers to access from the advertisements the information they held in memory.

Here endeth the psychology lesson...

As we close this mini-study on the way people perceive things, how are you feeling? Drained? Confused? Well, in case it's all too technical and complicated for you at this time, let's appreciate a wonderful and simple truth that should bring us all back down to earth:

Customers like the act of buying products and services.

Yes, people actually get a great deal of pleasure from just the experience of shopping in and of itself, regardless of the emotional benefits obtained from the products ultimately purchased. In other words, the purchasing experience can be the main emotional benefit.

Most research to do with shopping experiences has been carried out in retail store environments, where emotional benefits include a sense of adventure, socialising with others while making selections, self-gratification and perceived value. But there's no reason to limit the boundaries of emotional benefits to retail or any other market sector. Whether you are in a business-to-consumer market or business-to-business, people all have the same perceptual processing system, even if they don't all share identical likes and dislikes.

That's why your brand experience – the total set of interfaces with the customer – should be as carefully controlled as possible. The customer is out there waiting – and wanting – to take part in that positive experience. Let's not disappoint. Turn the page and find out how to influence perception to the maximum.

4

Making sense of the senses

There is no way in which to understand the world without first detecting it through the radar-net of our senses.

Diane Ackerman

5

Foreground and background

In the previous chapter we learned that in order to evoke emotion, we need to influence perception. We also covered the fact that perception incorporates at least the five 'traditional' senses: sight, sound, smell, taste and touch. Yet how many businesses really exploit all five? In my experience the focus has mostly been on sight only. Brochures, fliers, direct mail, advertisements – all designed to create a visual impression for the customer.

That's fine as it stands (although differentiation purely by visual means is getting more difficult by the day). But what about the other four senses? To limit a brand experience to just one out of five opportunities means missing 80 per cent of the influencing power! This is hardly the most intelligent way to build a powerful brand experience. Sadly, most small businesses simply neglect to include multiple senses in even their basic areas of operation.

> Senses drive perception, which evokes emotion.

We need to emphasise the importance of incorporating as many senses as we can in the customer experience, so let's establish a 'golden rule' about their use:

> The more senses you can engage in your customer experience, the more powerful it will be – and the greater the chances of your brand moving into long-term memory.

Of course, not every sense can be made available at each customer interface. The point, however, is that the richer and more intense experiences are the ones most likely to make it on the trek to long-term memory. As we'll also discover in the chapters on innovation in Part 5, when it comes to building your Brand Halo™ not every activity and process your business carries out is necessarily that important to the customer in terms of perception.

Some points of contact are obviously needed in your business and therefore attention needs to be paid to incorporating combined sensory activity. Other areas of your business, however, may not ever concern the customer because they are a back office, or a warehouse, or some other 'invisible' side to your operation. (That doesn't mean that your staff who work in these places should be faced with dull, dingy, demotivating surroundings. Sensory perception is as critical for the people who work for you as it is for your customers.)

The point here is that you need to determine the key areas in which you'll concentrate and focus the maximum amount of time, effort and expense into creating powerful influencers of perception. In many cases you get to decide what you want your customer to experience and when. It's what I call the '*foreground and background separation*' of perceptual influence. Take a look at the simple diagram shown in Figure 5.1.

Figure 5.1   A vase, or two faces? Which do you see?

What do you see? Some of you reading this will immediately say, 'It's a white vase, set against a black background.' At the same time, other readers will say, 'It's a silhouette of two faces looking at each other.' Perhaps you saw only the vase and then when you had read about the two faces you saw those as well. Or vice versa.

Our brain forces what we perceive through our senses into two basic scenes: the foreground, which is what our eyes focus on; and a background, which is basically everything else. You might be able to alternate your focus between the foreground and background, so you see either one image or the other, but trying to see both images at the same time is very difficult, and with some scenes nigh on impossible.

Understanding this gives us another key point through which to build our optimum customer experience:

Decide which elements of your business need to be in the foreground. Keep all other elements in the background.

We'll see in the Brand Halo™ chapter (Chapter 13) that the foreground items are part of a Brand Reflection, but for now let's just ensure that we see the potential disaster of being unfocused in our service offering, giving the customer both foreground and background activity that together create a tangled mess of sensory confusion.

Think of it this way: have you ever been to a theatre or stage show or play that you really enjoyed? If the production and direction were handled correctly, your focus was entirely on the stage, its cast and characters, the lighting, music, sound effects, scenery and so on. Perhaps there were visual effects such as people appearing to fly from one side of the stage to the other. Where was your focus? Was it on the sound-mixing desk and crew, possibly located at the back of the hall, or in a booth somewhere? Was it on the mass of wires, cables, lighting boxes, spotlights and the hundreds of other props, electronics and technology responsible for actually bringing you the show? Of course not. But how much would your enjoyment have suffered if, say, every time a flying sequence was due to take place, the curtain was pulled back and you saw several people manipulating the wires and pulling all kinds of levers? Even when there's a need for a total scene change, the producers have the sense to bring the curtain down so all is hidden from view until they are ready for 'curtain up' and the new scene to begin. In other words, they know specifically what they want you to see – ie the foreground – and they also know what they want to keep 'invisible' in the background.

To create the best customer experience, make sure you know exactly where you want the focus to be at any given time. With that in mind, let's consider the five senses in turn.

6

Looking like your brand

What does your customer experience look like? Is it attractive, compelling, emotive? What makes the visual elements of your company intense enough to place the experience into the shrine of the brand god: long-term memory? This is not a book on design, whether it be about products, graphics, advertising, logos or website design. There are literally hundreds of books out there that cover those subjects in great detail and I don't intend to reinvent the wheel. What we are concerned about here are some of the basic principles that need to be considered to ensure that the sum of all your visual items can be used to influence perception.

I've already mentioned that businesses usually focus on the visual sense – what people can see. So, a company that only has sight as a sensory influence is operating in a very overcrowded arena. Who hasn't experienced the flood of daily junk mail, delivered by post or electronically, no sooner received than trashed? Drive down any street and you'll see hundreds of visual signs, symbols, hoardings, posters and a multitude of images all begging us for attention. Try watching your favourite television programme without being interrupted by advertisers clambering over each other to get noticed. Businesses know all too painfully that the vast majority of this constant barrage of visual material doesn't have any staying power and never makes it past our short-term memory store.

All too often we see these attempts at capturing our attention as isolated, fragmented incidents. But a vital key to creating a strong visual experience is consistency. The most important aspect of influencing the visual sense is

Figure 6.1 Kanizsa's triangle

that there must be consistency in how the brand is presented. Take a look at the illustration in Figure 6.1.

This is known as Kanizsa's triangle, after the Italian psychologist who created it. Most people will see a white triangle in front of the three black circles – but it doesn't actually exist. Rather, it is 'invented' by your brain, which likes to observe patterns. If there's a pattern to be made, the brain will make it. If not, the brain will simply view each element as a separate entity, with no real connection. This leads us nicely to an important principle of influence through the visual sense:

Customers are influenced the most when there is a consistent pattern to the visual sensory materials used.

Just to reinforce this concept, take a look at the picture in Figure 6.2. What do you see?

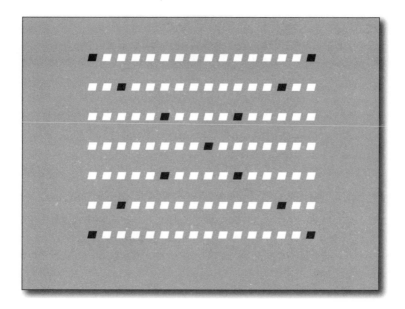

Figure 6.2   Our brain recognises patterns

Although the illustration is composed only of white and black dots, the arrangement of the black dots is such that we see a pattern – in fact, we create one. So, how is this related to our visual branding stimuli? Well, if you think about your array of visual materials as the black dots, what can you do to ensure there is consistency and the formation of a pattern in what the customer sees?

Visual influence works with a number of important facets: colour, shape, space, size, placement, tone and even typography. How much your visual brand wows those who experience it will be down to how consistently these visual ingredients are used.

This is where a well-constructed visual identity manual comes to the fore. A visual identity manual is a guidebook on how to ensure the brand is always seen in a consistent manner, and describes how active visual branding tools such as leaflets, brochures, advertisements, websites, presentations, packaging and so on, and passive reminders such as uniforms, vehicle liveries and signage, will be used to create strong, identifiable patterns of visual stimuli.

Creating a visual brand identity

Visual identity is a highly subjective area. Consider the use of colour, for example. What is a preferred colour to one person is a turn-off to another. Do you like red? Red can represent power, heat and passion – but it can also mean danger and warnings. What about yellow? The colour yellow can suggest the sun, summer, happy times… or it can be the colour of cowardice, or the prohibition of parking or some other traffic issue.

Virgin clearly has no problem with the colour red for its logo, and supporters of the Virgin brand would consider emotions such as passion and power quite relevant. And what about the Coca-Cola symbol? It isn't Virgin, but its logo is red and has its own unique set of emotional values to portray. As for yellow – well, in the years I spent consulting for Yellow Pages, no negative connotations ever came up in market research or customer feedback about the colour.

Then we get into the realms of colour combinations. What about red and yellow together? Does that combination have connotations of both danger and cowardice? Hmm… I don't think McDonald's has ever thought about ditching its famous 'arches' logo of red and yellow just in case people misconstrue what it stands for. The Red Cross, on the other hand, uses red to convey a totally different meaning. Created in 1863 as a red cross on a white armband to identify medics on a battlefield, the symbol was used by its armed forces members. But although its colour has not created problems, its shape certainly has. The red cross design was originally based on the Swiss flag, with its colours reversed. This idea was not welcomed by people in Muslim countries, who saw the design as representative of the medieval religious Crusades against non-Christian nations, so the Red Crescent was adopted in the 1930s as the Muslim symbol within the International Committee of the Red Cross.

In December 2005, another new symbol – the Red Crystal – was introduced as a universally acceptable symbol for relief workers in states objecting to both the cross and the crescent on religious grounds.

There are many complex reasons why different emblems have been utilised within the Red Cross organisations around the world. But emotional issues appear to be behind every symbol. Perhaps it is fair to say, then, that the colour itself is not the main bone of contention. Rather, it's what the symbol represents in terms of perception.

The same is true for any business logo or visual identity. Clearly, what's most important is not just the colour but how the colour is used, and how it fits within the customer experience as a whole. Consider these points:

■ Is the colour linked to a negative situation in your business market, so that undesirable emotions will be evoked when it is seen by your customers?
■ Is the shape of the logo or symbol similar to something else that might not generate positive emotions?

Like all other elements of visual identity, it is the context in which they are used that will determine their relevancy. We've just seen that religious differences can cause even well-established emblems to be reconsidered. Other factors, such as cultural differences and superstitions, can also have a major impact on the acceptance or rejection of a certain colour, too. Professor J L Morton, a leading expert in colour theory, recounts the problems Disney had with signage when its Euro Disney theme park in Paris was launched. Disney's signs used large amounts of purple – a colour quite common on signs in its US sites – which visitors found 'morbid' because in Catholic Europe, purple is a symbol of death and crucifixion. (Professor Morton has an excellent website at www.colormatters.com that tells you everything you'll ever need to know about colour.)

Good design... or bad design? Who chooses?

Creating a good visual identity really does need someone with an eye for design. I've seen many instances in small businesses where, because the office computer comes complete with 250 typefaces, almost every one of them gets used! Colour schemes are often based on what the business owner likes personally (apparently Euro Disney's signage catastrophe happened because the CEO liked purple – yet purple is often used as a signage colour in Disney's US parks), and advertising material is usually built around gimmicks or a style of humour the proprietor finds funny, even if no one else does. In other words, it's about as customer-unfocused as you can get.

In May 2007 the official logo for the London 2012 Olympic Games was launched amid a huge wave of criticism, anger and outrage. Costing in the region of £400,000 and designed by the world-famous design consultancy Wolff Olins, the logo was meant to depict the date 2012 and used pink, blue, green and orange colours. Opposition to the logo came not only from the general public but from the design industry, too. Graphic designers accused Olins of using old-fashioned typography and confusing patterns. Others felt that the logo needed extensive explanations as to its meaning, which didn't engender public support. Some protestors likened the logo to a swastika, while others described it as Lisa Simpson. Most descriptions were derisive to say the least.

Interesting that Lord Sebastian Coe, chair of the organising committee, felt that the logo was 'the vision at the very heart of our brand'. So strong was the feeling that Wolff Olins had got it wrong that an internet-based petition was set up, attracting many thousands of signatures.

Was this just about a design, or did it go deeper than that? Did the British public feel embarrassed or foolish about the way London's flagship investment was being depicted? Just how much was about design – and how much to do with emotion?

It's somewhat reminiscent of the 1997 debacle when British Airways did away with its famous 'Speedbird' logo and replaced it with tail-fin emblems designed by international artists, intending to represent the various countries to which BA flew its passengers. Each aircraft also carried the name of that particular country on the rear of the fuselage. The public outcry at the seeming overt move away from its British roots was huge.

Even Margaret Thatcher, Prime Minister at the time, expressed her absolute disapproval of the designs, covering one of the tailfins with her handkerchief and declaring, 'We fly the British flag, not these awful things.' By 2001, BA had repainted its fleet with a stylised version of the Union Jack and regained its customers' approval. Commentators at the time noted that the 'pride of the British public was hurt'.

Emotions, again, led the nationwide outrage. It wasn't the design *per se*; it was the meaning behind it. These two accounts should alert you to the fact that no logo, typeface or design can exist in isolation from the customer. Find out as much as you can about your customers' likes and dislikes and what drives them. After all, when you're building a powerful brand the last thing you want is a rebellion on your hands.

Ideally, if you want to create a compelling visual experience, you should hire the services of a graphic design company whose designers know how to put together visual identity programmes.

Unfortunately, the cost of consultants is often more than a small business can afford – but that shouldn't mean all is lost. You could enlist the services of a local designer or even a student on a graphic design course to help with getting the consistency right. You're not commissioning a multi-million-pound/dollar logo that's only ever printed in gold on pure silk (unless you're selling to customers who buy very expensive silk items, or aiming your business at customers who would expect to see nothing less than a lavish identity) but a workable, fully aligned set of visual elements that the customer can follow and make sense of.

In fact, as far as logos are concerned, it's arguable that for the average business a black dot on a white piece of paper would do just fine as a logo – as long as it reflected what the business stood for, met the criteria discussed earlier with regard to accepted cultural, societal and business symbols, and did it in a consistent manner.

If you've got the money, then a graphic design consultancy will give you a logo and accompanying designs for your collateral, website and so on that will certainly bring your overall identity to the front of stage – and there is indeed a time and place for that to happen (like when you're rich and famous and your 50-strong marketing department is telling you it's time for a rebrand). But the most important element of the whole customer experience is consistency, and as long as you put that in place first, the fineries can wait. Of course, if your overall image is out of date or looks absolutely awful, then maybe you'll need to start work on the identity a lot earlier. After all, we want to be consistent... but not consistently bad.

The critical thing with all visual requirements is to ensure that whoever has the responsibility to create the visual identity, whether in-house or external supplier, is given a full and comprehensive brief. You've heard the old saying, 'Garbage in, garbage out', and that's never been more true than of businesses who give a bad brief to a designer and expect nothing short of design work comparable to the ceiling of the Sistine Chapel to be produced. You own the concept of what you want your visual customer experience to look like. Don't expect the designer to own this for you. His or her job is one of translation: to take the information you have provided, including your passion and vision for how you want your business to be viewed, and translate it into tangible signs, symbols and elements that reflect the image you want to portray.

What is the Nike 'swoosh' logo worth? Billions, no doubt. So, how much did it cost to create the famous logo representing the wing of the Greek goddess Nike? In 1971, Nike co-founder Phil Knight paid Carolyn Davison, a graphic design student at Portland State University, just $35 to design it – and he didn't even like it at first! In 1983, Phil Knight gave Carolyn a diamond ring engraved with the swoosh, and an undisclosed sum of Nike stock as a belated thank-you for creating what was to become one of the most recognised symbols in the world.

The sights your customers see should help evoke memories, feelings, opinions – in fact, anything and everything that will lead to an intense impression passing through the perceptual processing system. Strong images, photographs and illustrations linked to your business and its products and services can help build a powerful visual identity. Remember, you're not building your customer experience along purely rational lines, so design elements that pander only to product or service features are simply not good enough. Use imagery in the way that a painter uses paint, or a photographer uses the camera, to elicit responses that go way beyond the tangible and the norm.

For example, the logo shown in Figure 6.3 for an Italian food delivery service is designed to evoke the pleasure of enjoying fine Italian pasta, while conveying a sense of fun and frivolity. This overall feeling can be applied to all other aspects of the business, such as uniforms, packaging, delivery bikes and so on.

Figure 6.3 Visual identity. Courtesy of Motive Design, London

Contrast this to the advertisement shown in Figure 6.4 for a non-profit organisation dealing with hunger in a drought-ridden area of the Third World. The image is stark; it reflects the plight of starving people without being overly shocking.

How much could this type of imagery be carried over to other aspects of the organisation's activity? Certainly items like flyers, mailers, the website, slide presentations, exhibition stands, short films and other awareness-building components could utilise complementary visual imagery. Even the organisation's reception area could carry large black-and-white pictures that have been used in these other areas to great effect. Again, the point is to create an identifiable pattern of visual stimulation.

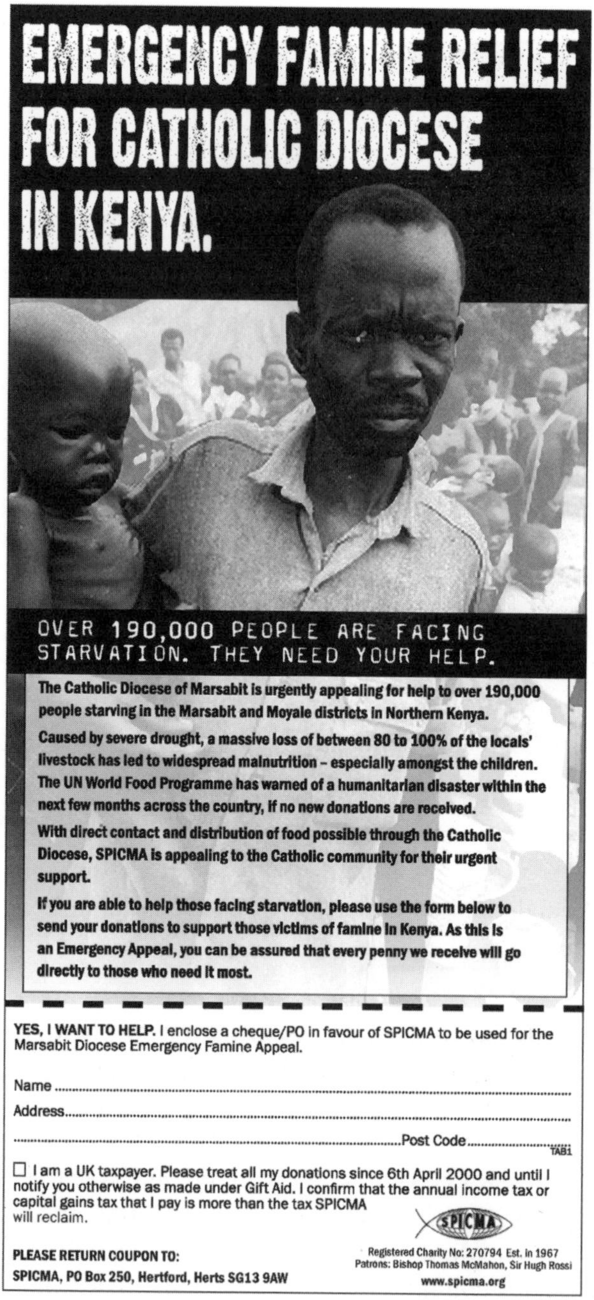

Figure 6.4 Eliciting customer responses through imagery: advertisement by a non-profit organisation. Reproduced with permission of SPICMA

Visual identity manuals can range from a few succinct pages relating to the most important parts of the sight sense, to hundreds of pages detailing to the nearest millimetre where the company logo should be placed. How far you want to go in defining your overall visual experience will depend on the type of business you are in and how many different aspects of your company the customer is likely to see. Specifications and guidelines should therefore be created to provide the optimum customer experience only in relevant areas.

If you use the services of an external designer, make sure that she or he understands the boundaries of the manual. That means the building blocks of your visual approach should acknowledge that there are foreground and background parts of your operation. That's why we're not talking here about creating some kind of 'integrated marketing' handbook. No business has all of its ducks in a row (and doesn't need to, as you'll discover in Part 5 of the book, on innovation). The ones that are in the foreground – in other words, the areas that your customers deem important – should be the point of focus for your identity manual.

For example, if your staff are heavily engaged in face-to-face meetings with customers, how do they look? Do they wear uniforms, or some other identifying feature such as a badge – or do they carry a particular type of briefcase or folder? If this aspect of your customer service is more in use than, say, advertising in the local newspaper, don't spend time and money detailing in your manual how the logo in an ad must always be indented from the top left-hand corner by a certain fixed measure. Instead, create proper guidelines on the manner of dress, or what accessories will be used at all times.

Your reception area

What does your reception area look like? Does it take advantage of the many visual cues that can be used to enhance the customer experience? Consider these elements:

- Does it have an easel or board with a welcome notice personalised for the customers who are visiting you, or do you just rely on the receptionist to greet them?
- Are there well-maintained plants on display that enhance the reception area surroundings, together with appropriate lighting and wall displays that all work together to give the customer the best view of your business at that contact point?

- Are there proper coat hangers for your customers' outerwear, or are they expected to throw their coats over the back of the reception furniture?
- Is there a clock on the wall and perhaps even a flat-screen monitor running your business presentations, or news updates on your products or services?
- Are your logo and signage clearly visible and do they create an impact and a focal point for the visitor?

It isn't unusual for me to arrive at a reception desk having literally to climb over several boxes of items that a courier has dropped off and no one has yet cleared from the floor. En route, it's quite common to see tropical plants caked with dust and various insects, partially concealed by waste-paper baskets full of empty paper cups from the drinks dispenser. Various business magazines and newspapers, all out of date, litter the reception table. What do I see? I see a mess... and that's the visual customer experience I take away with me.

The visual appeal of a reception area is of paramount importance to those businesses involved in therapy, dental healthcare markets. Chances are, clients won't get to see a clinician immediately. What can they do while they're waiting? Are there visual elements designed to put them at ease, such as appropriate pictures or illustrations? Much as it might interest you, most of your clients don't want to see pictures of internal organs, rotting teeth or ingrown toenails. Far better to show positive images designed to relax patients rather than scare them. Are there educational materials to scan, so that clients can learn a little more about your area of clinical practice?

Do you have your own promotional items visible and accessible? Are magazines and newspapers appropriate to your practice – or do clients turn the page only to read an article completely opposed to your clinical approach?

A friend of mine went for her regular dental check-up and was going to enquire about having her teeth whitened. The first magazine she picked up in the reception area carried a lengthy article on the dangers of tooth whitening, along with pictures of victims of over-bleached teeth and gums. Despite the fact that the article was referring to some over-the-counter tooth-whitening kits and emphasised that carried out by a professional it was a safe process, the article was enough to deter her from even discussing it with the dentist.

Your office environment

What about the offices themselves? Are your staff forced to work in less than desirable visual surroundings, with only an occasional plastic plant and cheap picture thrown in to make the ambience more appealing? Old desks, worn-out chairs and threadbare carpets won't be key motivators for your workforce, either. Studies have shown that a pleasant office environment leads to happier employees who have lower stress levels and cooperate better with their colleagues – all of which has a significant impact on their daily productivity.

All of this needn't cost an arm and a leg. Decent, appropriate furnishings are available at very reasonable cost nowadays. Of course, if you rarely come into personal contact with your client base and instead deal mainly through your website, direct mail or advertising campaigns, then reception areas and offices might be considered background, not foreground, issues. Thus, the focus will be better placed on producing a detailed specification of graphic layouts and design. Understand, however, that there is a difference between a background item not being the focus, and its being neglected altogether. It's horses for courses. Just don't forget why you're doing this (because you want your brand to take up residence in the customer's long-term memory). If your staff's working conditions are ignored, then a key aspect of your brand will be at risk.

One word of caution. Don't make your visual identity manual a committee project. Give it to the external consultants and let them get on with it, or, if money is tight, assign someone to be the project leader, with the remit that if the manual accurately covers the visual facets that are deemed important, then the job is done. Remember the old saying: 'A camel is a horse designed by a committee.' The only thing that will happen if a committee gets hold of it is that any original creativity will be squeezed out by personal opinions. You'll never accommodate everyone's views, because they are so subjective.

And don't ask the customers what they think, either. Why? Because, as we've seen, they too are diverse in their likes and dislikes. I keep coming back to the main point that what we're after is the *total customer experience*. When you know what your customers – as a group, social 'tribe' or cluster – like and dislike, and when you put into place a consistent, uniform set of customer-focused experiences that can be seen as a strong pattern because it matches their emotional needs and wants, then you'll stand the best chance of pushing your brand into long-term memory.

What's in a name?

You'll notice that I haven't spent any time discussing the ins and outs of coming up with a brand name. There is an awful lot of nonsense paraded about as 'brand expertise' in areas such as creating and researching logos, brand names and so on.

Some so-called brand experts will devote entire chapters of their books to stressing the importance of getting the brand name right. Because of patents and copyright laws, brand names do have to be checked out from a legal viewpoint. And if your brand is going to be global, you don't want your name to mean something stupid or inappropriate in another country or language.

But when it comes to determining what is a 'right' brand name, who's to say what's correct and not correct? Research of this kind may well be an expensive red herring – and unnecessary. After all, just think of some of the strange-sounding brand names that exist. Who'd suppose they could ever be the result of asking the public what they thought? For example, in the United Kingdom one of the best-selling household cleaning products is called Cillit Bang (known in the United States, Canada, and Australia as Easy-Off BAM). Cillit Bang? What in the world is that all about? Was this name the result of some amazingly detailed market research spread over many years involving hundreds of focus groups? Were 'sensible' names like 'Wipe-off' or 'Acme-Kleen' rejected by panels of philosophers and psychologists in favour of something more intellectually demanding?

On the contrary, the company that makes it, Reckitt Benckiser, was already marketing a range of wax polishes called Cillit in Europe. Apparently, the word 'Bang' was simply added by the CEO to describe the product's cleaning power.

'Nuff said.

Use technology to your advantage

Modern technology has opened up the whole visual sense with the advent of websites, CD and DVD presentations, mobile phones and other places where visual stimuli can be used to give a positive brand advantage. We live in a multimedia world, so even for the smallest business, creating items such as professional-looking slide shows, e-books and short movies that can be mailed out to clients on CVs or DVDs as well as being accessible from the company's website is getting to be a basic requirement.

The key point here is not about how much technical wizardry you can incorporate into creating your customer experience but about how it is used to influence the visual image of your business in the strongest way. Let's take the humble electronic slideshow that seems to take pole position in business meetings today. When making a presentation, do you simply create one slide after another crammed full with bullet points or lengthy paragraphs of text, all repeating word for word what you are going to be saying? Is that emotive? Hardly. It's a guaranteed way, though, to lose your target audience very early on in the proceedings, as so many presenters do. A better way is to have just one or two bullet points on each slide, along with exciting imagery, and use the slides to complement what you are saying, not repeat it. (Check out www. eyefulpresentations.co.uk for some comprehensive information on how to make effective presentations.)

These same presentation principles apply to any small movie you make for your customers. We're not trying to equal Tarantino's work, or create another Superman movie, but we are trying to create maximum visual influence. Here are some key points to consider:

- What is your movie about? Is it a product or service demonstration? Is it an explanation of something about your business?
- Does it focus only on features and tangible benefits, or does it incorporate emotional triggers?
- How much can be understood purely by the visual content? One way of determining the power of the visual side of things is to turn the sound off. Is what you see exciting, does it inspire, move, delight, encourage… in other words, from a visual standpoint, does it work? Get this aspect right and you can have a really powerful visual tool in your brand toolbox.

This section has dealt with some very basic principles that all too often are missing or inadequate in the visual arena of a business, and we've discussed the importance of what your identity looks like. In the next chapter we'll consider the other vital aspect of your brand's sight sense: your personal image (and that of your staff). Here, we'll consider the two main areas of attention: first, how you appear in terms of dress; and second, how you come across to your audience with regard to body language.

7

Your BodyBrand™

Today we live in a fashion-conscious world. There is no longer a 'one-way-only' business dress style. In the 1990s the idea of 'dressing down' led to many businesses opting for the smart casual approach of khakis and polo shirts, tank tops and halter necks, in preference to executive suits and outfits. But this trend seems to be reversing. According to a survey carried out in the United States by the Society for Human Resource Management in 2005, only 41 per cent of US companies allowed casual dress.

Whether or not you choose to dress casually or formally is not the issue. What matters (as always) is how consistent you appear in your overall personal image, how your staff's image is aligned with it, and how relevant it is to the kind of customer you deal with. Do your customers care about how you dress? Have you asked them? Have you assumed that informal dress is OK simply because other companies favour it or allow it, or because it's your own preference?

One other consideration: uniforms. As any airline knows, a uniform is a major customer talking point and a very high attention-getting part of its brand, which is why many airlines, along with retail chains and others who have uniforms as part of the corporate dress codes, employ top designers to create distinctive and stylish outfits. Not every business needs a uniform. But a distinctive style of dress – whether that means a casual T-shirt emblazoned with the company logo, or a smart executive suit in your visual identity colour – can create a unique differentiation if you decide to incorporate it.

In one graphic design consultancy I took over, the client service managers all dressed in very individual styles, from smart business attire to a totally casual approach. When I put the idea forward that we ought to introduce a uniform look, there was immediate uproar. 'We're not airline cabin crew,' said one defiant female. 'We don't work in a supermarket,' responded two of the guys, heads nodding in agreement all round the table.

For a brief moment it looked as though I'd have a mass walkout on my hands. 'No one is asking you to wear that kind of uniform,' I replied calmly. 'I'm thinking more about creating a very upmarket, smart and confident image. How about if I gave all the men Armani suits and the women outfits from Donna Koran?' I asked quite openly. 'Then things like company ties, scarves, cufflinks and jewellery could all be used as the coordinating items.'

There was a short period of silence, followed by whispers of 'Armani... Donna Karan...' Then one of the female managers looked at me and said, 'How soon do we start with this new image?'

Of course, whatever dress code you employ, proper grooming is a must. Looking good in terms of dress sense is one thing; how your own personal behaviour is displayed is something else. If a powerful brand stands out from the crowd because of its difference in perception, you (and your staff) will be a central cog in the wheel, especially if you are dealing with customers face-to-face on a regular basis.

Visual communication – up close and personal

Unlike other visual identity materials, which have been created to a brief, you have arrived with your image already in place! The question is, how well does it come across to others, particularly your customers? Bear in mind that we communicate both verbally and non-verbally, and aspects such as facial expressions, gestures, posture and eye contact strongly affect how you and your employees – and therefore the brand – are perceived.

Of course, with non-verbal messages making an impression, it's impossible not to communicate even if you are not actually speaking! So, whether you are seen as a negative or positive brand representation will depend upon how well you use positive non-verbal elements along with the words you speak. Note that we're not trying to second-guess the body postures and expressions of the customer here. We're talking about your own gestures and stances, along with those of the employees you may have.

Have you been caught out by the claim that our communication spectrum is split up into three isolated parts: voice, intonation and body language? Have you also been told that actual words represent only 7 per cent of our overall communication, while intonation (tone of voice, pitch, etc) represents 38 per cent, leaving body language the key influencer at a staggering 55 per cent? Don't believe it, because it's not true.

In 1972 the researcher Albert Mehrabian conducted some experiments dealing with the communication of feelings and attitudes, particularly those relating to someone saying they liked or disliked something, at the same time giving the opposite impression by their tone of voice and body language. The 7–38–55 percentage split was the result of that rather specific test. Somehow these figures became an all-encompassing set of 'facts' about the communication spectrum that has spread across the globe, being taught in many schools and universities and by a whole gamut of business teachers and trainers.

Mehrabian himself has stated that he never intended his results to be applied to normal conversation as a universal statement. The idea that only 7 per cent of our communication is verbal under any conditions is quite ridiculous. If it were true, learning Russian or Chinese in one evening would be a cinch, as pronouncing words wouldn't really matter that much provided we used the right body language.

Like so many models and ideas in marketing and branding that are based on false assumptions, this one needs to be trashed. Yes, body language and vocal intonation are very important and can have a significant impact on what is being said. It's true that sometimes a shrug of the shoulders, the rolling of eyes or an extreme facial gesture can say a great deal without a word being spoken, but they must be seen in the context of the whole communication process that's taking place. Communications is about all three facets of communication: body language, intonation and words – and words play the greatest part.

Most of the time, it's impossible to determine another person's reason for adopting a particular stance or body position. The idea that customers who fold their arms are on the defensive or getting ready to become aggressive is far too dogmatic and has no factual basis. It may be true sometimes, but not in every instance. I often fold my arms when I'm talking to a company representative – and so might you – simply because it's comfortable, not because I want a fight. Well, not usually...

Seeing eye to eye with your customers

However, while your task here is not to analyse the customer's non-verbal language, you'd better believe that they are analysing yours. To any customer, there are general aspects of body language that can be perceived in a better light than others.

For example, when you meet a customer, do you adopt good eye contact, which communicates to the customer that you are pleased to see him or her (you are pleased, aren't you?) or do you look away, or down at the floor, and take on a facial expression that implies the customer is something of an intrusion into your day?

Research has shown that eye contact is very important in establishing positive feelings about a company representative, whereas lack of eye contact increases distrust. Good eye contact, however, does not mean staring intently at the customer without any break. Some people are naturally shyer than others and tend to maintain eye contact for much shorter periods of time.

One of the best guides to establishing appropriate eye contact is to watch the client's own eye contact time. Don't mirror and don't copy, but if the customer tends to look away often, you might want to maintain eye contact for shorter periods throughout the conversation. If, on the other hand, the customer continues eye contact for longer periods, you can lengthen the periods of your own eye contact with confidence.

Studies within the field of psychology have also suggested that smiling represents one of the most powerful non-verbal cues in the communication spectrum. The research conducted showed that people who smiled throughout a conversation were seen as exhibiting more warmth than those who smiled only infrequently. Even if the customer is angry about a particular matter, smiling at both the start and the end of the conversation is still a 'must do'. Customers retain the 'end frames' of a conversation more than any other part of the communication that took place.

Standing up (or sitting down) for your brand

What about posture? If you are seated, do you slouch, suggesting to the customer that you are tired, uninterested or bored, or do you sit upright and attentive, indicating that you are pleased to be doing business? How about where you stand when you discuss things with a client? Is your body position facing the client or is it sideways on? This particular stance, along with leaning back or stepping away from the customer, basically says 'your time is up', so unless you really want to get rid of the customer, don't give this visual impression.

Here's a better position to take. When having a conversation with the customer, lean forward slightly. If you're seated, then position yourself near the edge of the chair rather than pushed into the back. And if you're behind your desk, rest your hands on the desktop in front of you.

Respecting the personal space of customers is also a crucial part of a positive brand experience. Do you invade their personal space or do you respect the fact that customers, especially those of the opposite sex to you, do not want an in-your-face experience? Personal space zones vary from culture to culture and person to person. Find out what is right for your customers and your market.

Handshakes from hell

And let's not forget the killer of all positive customer experiences: the handshake. Most customers either find themselves at the receiving end of a bone-crushing encounter or feel as though they've just been handed a floppy wet fish to hold. A handshake should be firm enough to convey enthusiasm but not so firm that it hurts the client! If in doubt, do a handshake test with a colleague. (But make sure the other person knows how to give a good handshake first. Good handshakes, believe it or not, are few and far between.)

What about hand and head gestures? Do you stand like an inanimate dummy when engaged in conversation with a client? Or do you use occasional nods to give positive confirmation that you are listening to what is being said? Do you use other gestures when discussing aspects of your product or service, creating emphasis and demonstrating enthusiasm and knowledge, or do you simply spit out sentence after sentence, expecting the customer to take it all in?

Then there are those annoying habits that customers can get really angry about. For example, the company representative might continually tap a pen or other object on the desk, or beat out some strange drumbeat with fingers or toes. Shuffling, fidgeting or sniffing repeatedly is enough to put the dampeners on any brand experience.

Give yourself a body check

These comments on using positive body language may appear to be common sense, but they certainly are not common practice. Yet seemingly small matters of how you stand and the kinds of expressions you use can make a huge difference to the way in which customers perceive you – and therefore your brand. The problem is, body language is often performed unconsciously. You do not usually decide exactly how you are going to stand, or what gesture you might use; you do it without thinking.

That doesn't mean, however, that you can't change bad posture or train yourself to use appropriate gestures and expressions that enhance the customer experience. But first you have to know where you are with these various elements of body talk. Use the following checklist to do an honest appraisal of where you need to improve. Get a partner or business colleague to rate your scores. And if you employ staff, give everyone a copy and make certain that any shortfalls in body language skills are dealt with.

There are hundreds of courses and some excellent books on body language and communication skills, so there's really no excuse for not giving customers a positive BodyBrand™ every time.

Checklist for non-verbal communication

Score: 1 = bad, 5 = excellent

Eye contact
I look directly at the customer when speaking and listening.
    1   2   3   4   5
My eye contact 'breaks' fit with the customer.
    1   2   3   4   5
If I am conversing with a group of customers, I divide my eye contact equally between them.
    1   2   3   4   5

Body position
I maintain an attentive standing position when talking with a customer.
    1   2   3   4   5
I maintain an attentive seated position when talking with a customer.
    1   2   3   4   5
I respect and maintain the customer's personal space.
    1   2   3   4   5
I stand facing the customer, not turned sideways.
    1   2   3   4   5
I lean slightly forward to show that I am engaged in the conversation.
    1   2   3   4   5

Facial expressions
I smile at the customer often, throughout the conversation.
    1   2   3   4   5
I use my eyes, eyebrows and forehead to reflect visually my understanding of the points the customer makes.
    1   2   3   4   5
My expressions convey appropriate empathy to match the mood of the customer.
    1   2   3   4   5

Gestures
I use appropriate gestures throughout my presentation or discussion with the customer to help emphasise key points.
    1   2   3   4   5

I use gestures to show customers where to walk, to beckon them to come forward or point out some visual item.

   1   2   3   4   5

My gestures usually involve my palms pointing upwards.

   1   2   3   4   5

Habits

I have eliminated the following habits when engaged in customer communication:

– Repeatedly clicking a pen or pencil.

   1   2   3   4   5

– Twisting or turning a pen, pencil or other object.

   1   2   3   4   5

– Tapping my fingers or my toes.

   1   2   3   4   5

– Playing with my hair or preening myself.

   1   2   3   4   5

– Other habits (you decide!):

	1	2	3	4	5
_____	1	2	3	4	5
_____	1	2	3	4	5
_____	1	2	3	4	5

8

Talking the walk

How well does your business speak to your customers – and listen to what they have to say? Customer service is a key differentiator for businesses, but you wouldn't think so when you read about the sorry tales told about businesses that 'don't listen, 'don't care' and almost, it would seem, go out of their way to be difficult with customers.

Given the amount of technology available to companies today, from off-the-shelf customer management software to full-blown purpose-built customer relationship management systems, you'd think that customer satisfaction would be at an all-time high. Yet the majority of customer surveys conducted over the past decade have shown a continual decline in the number of satisfied customers, with some studies showing that almost 70 per cent of customers who stop dealing with a particular company do so because of a perceived attitude of indifference the company displays towards them.

Is this why the proliferation of books and articles about customer care all seem to revolve around subjects like 'How to deal with an angry customer' or 'How to defuse a hostile customer situation'? Do we simply accept the fact that customers are usually unhappy about customer service and just learn ways to get over the problem? Wouldn't it be far more effective and healthy for our businesses to try to avoid having disgruntled customers in the first place?

Much of this dissatisfaction is the result of conversations with company representatives taking place over the small but powerful device known as the telephone. Actually, it starts even before the talking begins, because it's not uncommon to dial businesses whose phones ring for ages before anyone bothers to answer. Once you get through, the first people on the line are often those who haven't been trained to answer the telephone properly, or who have been instructed to respond with the most inept (and sometimes quite inappropriate) statements, such as 'Hi, I'm Tracey. How may I bring a smile to your face today?' Worse still, I've lost count of the number of times someone has told me that 'You've come through to the wrong department', as though it's my fault, when in fact it was the company's receptionist who put me through. And I've mentioned elsewhere in this book my contempt for companies that keep me on hold for ages and continually interrupt their own distorted, badly recorded music to tell me that my call is important. *They lie!*

To influence perception of the sound sense, we need to look at the two basic areas of sound your customers will hear: speech and music. Both are vital as independent aspects of the sound, but when they work together they provide a very powerful opportunity to create strong influences to plug into long-term memory. In this chapter we'll overview the key points of *talking your brand*.

SPEECH

Creating rapport with your customers

'Business? It's all about relationships' is a statement you'll often read in books on marketing and selling. The sentiment isn't necessarily wrong, but I don't believe that what customers are after is a relationship as such. Some books out there almost advocate an affair with the client, offering page after page of advice about 'loving' your customer, 'delighting your customer' and using other worn-out clichés in a vain attempt to teach customer service as some kind of seduction technique.

The fact is, however, that customers are not into that kind of stuff. They want to do business with you, not invite you to elope with them or be a part of their family. OK, some company executives socialise with their clients, whether it be on the golf course or at the restaurant. That's fine as far as it goes, but let's be realistic here: if you and your company goof enough times, then no matter how often you see your clients outside of work, you're going to lose the business – and so you should.

No, I don't think the main issue is about relationships. What customers really want is *rapport*. Although rapport is often equated with relationship, there is a subtle difference. 'Rapport' comes from the French word *rapporteur*, which means *to bring back* and is where we get the word 'reporter' from. Unlike a relationship, which concerns both parties' interests, beliefs, worldviews, etc, rapport – in our business context – is about 'bringing back' the customer's likes and dislikes and responding accordingly – once again putting the focus on the customer, not on ourselves.

As we've seen in a previous chapter, that doesn't mean forgoing all dignity and integrity when the obnoxious, rude person who's on the end of the line or in your face is a customer. Nor does it mean leaving every interesting and informative bit of information about yourself out of the conversation (customers appreciate a company representative's personality and the odd joke, and sometimes even like to know where you're going on holiday), but essentially the nature of rapport is about understanding the customer and being skilled enough in verbal communication to respond by saying the right thing at the right time.

How do we gain rapport? Contrary to what is stated in some books on selling and marketing, building rapport is not a crash course in overcoming customers' objections or trying to analyse their personality. Don't get me wrong. As we've already seen, body language and other aspects of non-verbal communication represent a big slice of our overall communication spectrum in context. But unless you're a mime artist, you don't want to rely on non-verbal communication alone to provide a great customer experience.

Rapport, in the verbal sense, sets out to achieve three main objectives:

■ creating a positive interaction with the customer;
■ building trust with the customer;
■ gaining long-term commitment from the customer.

As with all brand-building strategies, you won't get into long-term memory just through some occasional conversations with your customers. Brand experiences need to be built up, layer by layer as it were, with each layer reinforcing the one below it.

If you set the objectives for the speech part of your customer experience, then all employees, regardless of where they fit in your staff levels, can work to achieve them. And believe me, there are very few companies out there that really take the effort to establish rapport. The greeting I usually get from a receptionist or customer service contact is rarely said as though it is meant. As for building trust – well, I trust very few companies, simply because they've demonstrated many times over that they can't be trusted. Therefore, I am part of the ever-increasing number of customers who have little or no loyalty to many of the brands out there. So get this part right and yours will be a highly admired brand.

Studies have shown that customers may avoid purchasing a product or service, no matter how good it is, just because there is no rapport with the person or people who represent the company. At the same time, other studies show that when rapport has been established, it represents an accurate indicator of customer loyalty. This is in total agreement with the idea of putting the brand into long-term memory, because it's only when it arrives there that loyalty will be sustained.

Listen and respond

Many textbooks that teach techniques to improve the spoken word rely on very outdated approaches, such as the hierarchy of effects 'A-I-D-A' model discussed in Chapter 1. The idea is that through telling the customer about some aspect of your product or service you can gain their attention, and by elaborating on the features and benefits you can maintain their interest, leading to their desire for ownership and ultimately acting to acquire it.

But we know that people don't think in a linear manner, so this won't help our rapport-building skills at all. Neither will approaches that recommend flattering the client, or elevating the client's status, or making intimate remarks about age, gender or looks. Other authors might promote the concepts of 'mirroring' where you imitate, albeit in a very covert manner, elements such as the tone and pitch of the customer's voice.

When I trained as a psychotherapist, one of my earliest teachers was quite adamant that in order to get into rapport with clients we needed to mirror and reflect their body language and vocal components. At times, especially with patients who spoke very fast in a high-pitched voice and fidgeted constantly, it proved almost impossible to do.

After years in private practice, I've discovered that it makes no difference to the therapist–client relationship whether I mirror them or do entirely the opposite of what they do. In fact, some of my most successful client sessions have been when I was quite at odds with their vocal speed, tone and intonation, as well as with their body posture. At times, especially when a client is feeling down, the last thing I want to do is feel down as well; that's not empathy, nor is it therapeutic. But I don't want to jump up and down and whistle a happy tune either. What's important is rapport. You don't gain positive interaction and commitment by being a copycat. You do it by sensitivity and understanding.

Remember, clients want rapport, not ridicule.

The two ingredients of a customer conversation

To learn how to develop rapport, we need to understand an important aspect of socio-linguistics. But you'll be pleased to know that we don't need a huge psychology lesson this time, because the concept we'll utilise can be summed up very easily, as follows.

Customers have two critical components of conversation:

1. **'People personal' wants and needs.** This area of conversation is concerned with personal values, including dignity, pride, honour, self-esteem, competence and credibility. It may also take into account customers' desire for their families to have the same values accorded them.
2. **'Social personal' wants and needs.** This area is concerned with personal views on social inclusion or exclusion, fairness, rights, entitlements and equality. This has become one of the most important purchasing criteria in the past decade.

Notice how emotionally directed these components are. Both sections will be governed by all the issues we discussed in the chapter on emotion. People's conversation is always littered with worldviews, beliefs and opinions, because conversation plays out to others our own construct of the world around us. It stands to reason that when you or your staff converse with customers and what you say conflicts with either of these two elements, rapport deteriorates, often quite quickly.

If, on the other hand, you are able to sustain the customer-held values and beliefs – no matter how different they are from your own – then rapport levels will be maintained or even increase. I never cease to be amazed at how deficient company representatives are in this vital area of verbal communication, in both the words that are spoken and the approach taken.

Let me give you a personal example. Some time ago I received a direct mail piece through my door advertising a credit card with a very low interest rate. The promotion also included a free MP3 player, which looked good in the picture. So I filled in the paperwork and within a week my card arrived. So far, so good.

Then, three days later, I received another mailing from the same company offering the identical credit card but with an even lower rate of interest, plus a DVD player that was obviously worth considerably more than the small MP3 player in the original mailing. Confused, I telephoned the company. First I was kept in a call waiting queue for nearly five minutes, hearing repeatedly the all-too-common statement, 'All of our agents are busy right now, but please hold and someone will be with you shortly.'

This immediately contravened the personal wants and needs I have. I want to be treated with dignity, and, in my worldview, keeping me waiting (at my expense) is not good. I am being treated like some lifeless robot, not a human being. I finally managed to get through to an agent. She introduced herself by her first name and asked me how she could help. That's better. I'm now being treated with the respect I deserve.

Score so far? Not that high, I'm afraid, but she had a chance to turn it round. I then explained about the double mailing, and stated that I felt the second offer was better than the first, so I'd like to have the additional benefits applied to the card I'd just received. She put me on hold again. After a few moments, she returned and advised me that the second mailing was a mistake. 'You should never have received the second mailing, so I can only apologise.'

Now I'm really annoyed. The agent has told me that there is nothing that she can do, except to say sorry. My emotions are at full power. My personal values have been violated, simply because I no longer feel that I have credibility with this company. After all, if I did mean anything to them as a client, surely they could give me the better deal? It would appear not. In fact, they probably don't want me as a client. This is their way of telling me to get lost. I see mental images of television presenter Anne Robinson looking fiercely at me and exclaiming, 'You are the weakest link. Goodbye.'

Worse still, now my social values have been called into question, because I'm being told I shouldn't have seen the second mailing. Why not? Was I not good enough to qualify for the better deal? How was it fair that some people could have a different deal without any explanation as to why? My voice got louder and annoyance turned to anger. I insisted on speaking to a more senior person who could provide some answers. Two call transfers later (the first got through to the wrong department), I spoke to the Marketing Manager, who again apologised and said that for some unknown reason my name had been placed on the wrong database, so instead of being listed as an 'existing' card owner, I had been placed on the list to receive new mailings.

Hmm... it seemed a little incompetent, but we all make mistakes. So I accepted the apology and simply asked how best to swap the MP3 player in return for the DVD player, and when the lower interest rate would kick in. 'Oh, I'm afraid we can't do that, Sir,' came the reply. 'You see, this offer is for non-cardholders only. You already have a card, so we can't do that. The only thing you can do is to close your account with us, then open another one. But it's company policy that we can't issue a new card until six months after the previous account has been closed, so you still wouldn't be eligible for the offer.'

You might guess what happened in the end. You're right. I closed the account (I kept the MP3 player) and I vowed that I would never do business with that company again, even if they offered me 0 per cent interest for life. The process they had in place (ie mailing, forms, card sent out, etc) was very good. The rapport was simply non-existent.

Do you think my behaviour was unreasonable or over the top? If you do, let me say that you are in the minority. Thousands of people make up their minds every day to go elsewhere because even the most basic verbal communication with a business is flawed. This one hit the jackpot; I felt that I was let down in every way.

Reasons for customer contact

When you consider it, customers interface with a business verbally for a limited number of reasons, the usual ones being:

- to enquire about a product or service;
- to purchase a product or service;
- to chase a delivery;
- to ask for after-sales or technical support;
- to complain.

These reasons aren't restricted just to telephone contact. There are also face-to-face meetings and retail shopping moments of contact where rapport is still of the highest importance. Yet the problems associated with these customer interfaces are generally caused by the same disregard for the two core components of customer communications. (For example, I went shopping for a plain white shirt, but couldn't find any on the shelves. I asked the assistant where they were and he responded, 'I'm sorry, but we don't have them in white. But we've got them in blue.' I'll leave it to you to work out what people personal and social personal elements were ignored in that one.)

Also, how many shops have you been in where the minute you walk through the door, the salesperson says, 'Can I help you?' And how many times, in quick response, do you give the same answer: 'No thanks, I'm just looking?' Why is this crazy ritual perpetuated year in, year out? What's happening with the 'rules of engagement' here?

A friend who had just started work after leaving university bought himself a gift with his first month's salary: a flat-screen high-definition television with all the trimmings. In great anticipation he took it home and rigged it up, only to find that it didn't work properly.

Expecting trouble, he took his technically minded father with him back to the shop, where he explained the problem. As he proceeded to take the TV out of its box, the young store assistant stopped him. 'You don't have to show me the television. If you say it's faulty, it's faulty. I'm very sorry that we gave you something below standard. Now, would you like me to exchange it for another one that we can test here in the shop first, or would you prefer a refund?'

My friend (and his father) were so taken aback by this unusual level of customer care that they haven't stopped talking about it. They estimate that they've told at least a hundred people about 'the brilliant store' and have almost become non-salaried salespeople and ambassadors for the firm.

The assistant had been well trained. He understood people personal and social personal elements of conversation. He didn't make the customer feel bad, he didn't try to blame the customer and he acknowledged the company's own failings. He offered an apology but didn't waste time on sentiment. Instead, he moved swiftly on to offering the customer a choice.

At all times the customer's worldview was safe. Clients know that mistakes happen. Equipment fails. Problems arise. But that's rarely the reason they become unhappy with a company. It's how these problems are dealt with that determines the perception of the brand. For my friend and his father, it was handled well. The reward for the company is a place in their long-term memory.

Customer communication checklist

Rapport should not be difficult to achieve for business of any size. Much of it is about respecting the *people personal* and *social personal* conversation components and putting them into the context of the conversation. If you can do this, it will lead to a successful customer interaction. Here are a few general dos and don'ts:

- **Do create a Brand Lexicon**. Doing so is especially important for all customer-contact staff, but actually is a must for everyone in your business. A Brand Lexicon is a simple booklet (electronic or paper) containing key words, phrases and sentences that will be used when giving information to a customer. Like the visual identity manual, the Brand Lexicon will ensure that everyone in the company is using the same vocabulary and thus all are saying the same thing. This is vital if your company is dealing with technology or complex manufacturing issues.

   How often have you been talking to a company when a single product feature has been described not only differently but at times in almost a contradictory way by various salespeople or customer service agents? When this happens, customers might get confused about the proper description, but they get a clear message about the company: it's a shambles, so don't do business with it.

- **Don't make 'linguistic threats' to customers.** When you deny, ignore, argue with or disagree with the customer, you are essentially challenging both people personal and social personal constructs in his or her mind. You are, in essence, threatening their worldview, which is the one thing needed to make meaning of life. If you are dealing with irate customers, allow them to say what they need to say, to 'get it off their chest', then deal with the matter appropriately. The customer is looking for vindication, not a judgement. Make sure that you paraphrase what the customer tells you, and if it's a complicated issue, say it back to them so that they know you've been listening and that you fully understand the problem.

   Think about the two elements of customer communication at all times and assess which people personal and social personal aspects are being accessed. Reasonably accepting responsibility will often defuse a volatile situation. Remember, the customer isn't blaming you (unless it really was your fault). You're just the representation of the company in the customer's short-term memory system.

- **Do listen carefully to what the customer is saying and meet them at their current emotional level.** That means, if the client sounds subdued or is abrupt, don't respond by trying to change their mood. There's nothing worse, when you're having a bad day, than the company representative on the other end of the phone trying to engage in conversation about how lovely the weather is and how sweetly the birds are singing. Conversely, when the customer rings up in a happy, jolly frame of mind, avoid coming across with a depressed, tired, just-going-through-the-motions approach.

  And watch your tone of voice. It doesn't take a language expert to detect sarcasm, a condescending manner or sheer contempt, even if it's distanced by a telephone line. Frankly, if you can't be civil to a customer, what are you doing in that position? Much of this will be picked up by your tone of voice, which is easily transmitted down the telephone line even though the customer can't see you.

- **Don't make promises you can't keep.** Language communicates action as well as information. In other words, when you say that you'll do something, the customer expects you to do it, and rapport will deteriorate if you don't deliver on what you said. Issues such as failure to meet confirmed delivery dates and appointment times are often seen as a problem merely with the process side of the business and something the customer-facing staff can dismiss with a shrug of the shoulders, especially as it's often the responsibility of some other department to carry out the fulfilment side of things.

  But within verbal communication, making a promise actually performs the act of promising – rather like the minister who says, 'I now pronounce you husband and wife.' The 'promise' stated verbally is performed when it is stated. If you are in any doubt about your ability to make a promise, don't make it. Then go and sort out the faulty process that's preventing you from delivering for your customers. Remember that the majority of customer complaints are tied directly to things that have been done badly or not done as promised.

- **Don't say things like, 'You need to talk to someone else', or, 'You've come through to the wrong department.'** In either case it is not the fault – or concern – of the customer. Even if the customer did push the wrong button on the automated call service, you don't have to scold them. If you are going to transfer the call, why not check first to see if the right person's available, and if not, find some other employee responsible for the customer's query?

The most exasperating thing is when you get put through to a wrong department and they transfer you to someone's voicemail. Why can't they try the line first, then let you know the situation? Or hand you back to the switchboard and let them handle it? In fact, do anything except waste your time.

I received a mailer from a virtual telephone company offering 'personally answered calls', and as I was interested at the time, I decided to phone them up. Each time I phoned, the line was busy. Then, on the fourth attempt, I managed to get hold of one of the telephonists. I told her about the mailer, and she replied that she didn't know 'all the details' of the offer, and she'd get someone to ring me back later that day. Of course, no one did.

It was two days later when the apologetic owner phoned and told me how busy they had been that week and how she was still playing 'catch-up'. I made some small talk about how rushed things can get sometimes, then ended the call. Needless to say, I never used them. If that was how they handled inbound calls from their own potential clients, how confident could I be about them handling mine?

■ **Do use the customer's name as soon as you hear it, but don't keep repeating it before every sentence.** Whatever the sales gurus tell you, people don't want to be constantly reminded of who they are. And keep the conversation centred around the brand, not yourself. Include your company name as close to the beginning of the conversation as you can, then utilise appropriate key words or phrases from your Brand Lexicon often. This will give the caller memory cues to keep the brand alive throughout the discussions.

For example, if you contact Disney's call centre, the conversation they'll have with you will be replete with multiple uses of words like 'magic' and phrases such as 'the magic of Disney' and 'magical kingdom'. Chances are, you won't get off the phone without the word 'magic' still in your memory, albeit short-term. But put this together with the other experiences of 'Disney magic' you'll encounter at their parks and that place in long-term memory is almost assured.

Fifteen customer service no-nos

By Monte Enbysk, lead editor for the microsoft.com network. Reprinted with permission from the Microsoft Small Business Center at www.microsoft.com/smallbusiness.

Sometimes it seems like rude customer service is the rule rather than the exception. But there's rude – and then there's rude.

When it comes to getting customer service, what's your definition of rude? What unprofessional behaviour irritates you the most when, as a consumer, you are interacting by phone with another company?

Sometimes, customer service that is perceived as rude is not intentional and often is the result of absent-mindedness or carelessness on behalf of an employee. Either way, bad customer service can translate into lower sales and lost business, says Nancy Friedman, president and founder of the Telephone Doctor, a St. Louis-based customer service training company.

On the basis of its own surveys, the Telephone Doctor has compiled the 15 biggest sins of customer service employees today. They are listed below, along with the Telephone Doctor's guidelines (in parentheses) on how to do it right.

If your company's customer service managers and front-line employees are guilty of any of these, it's time for some action. Otherwise, you may have an image problem that could sabotage your effort to produce and market great products.

1. Your employees are having a bad day, and their foul mood carries over in conversations with customers. (Everyone has bad days, but customer service employees need to keep theirs to themselves.)
2. Your employees hang up on angry customers. (Ironclad rule: Never hang up on a customer.)
3. Your company doesn't return phone calls or voicemail messages, despite listing your phone number on your website and/or in ads and directories. (Call customers back as soon as you can, or have calls returned on your behalf.)

4. Your employees put callers on hold without asking them first, as a courtesy. (Ask customers politely if you can put them on hold; very few will complain or say 'No way!')
5. Your employees put callers on a speaker phone without asking them first if it is OK. (Again: ask first, as a courtesy.)
6. Your employees eat, drink or chew gum while talking with customers on the phone. (A telephone mouthpiece is like a microphone; noises can easily be picked up. Employees need to eat their meals away from the phone. And save that stick of gum for break time.)
7. You have call-waiting on your business lines, and your employees frequently interrupt existing calls to take new calls. (One interruption in a call might be excusable; beyond that, you are crossing the 'rude' threshold. Do your best to be prepared with enough staff for peak calling times.)
8. Your employees refuse or forget to use the words 'please', 'thank you' or 'you're welcome'. (Please use these words generously, thank you.)
9. Your employees hold side conversations with friends or each other while talking to customers on the phone, or they make personal calls on cell phones in your call centre. (Don't do either of these.)
10. Your employees seem incapable of offering more than one-word answers. (One-word answers come across as rude and uncaring.)
11. Your employees do provide more than one-word answers, but a lot of the words are grounded in company or industry jargon that many customers don't understand. (If you sell tech products, for example, don't casually drop in abbreviations such as APIs, ISVs, SMTP or TCP/IP.)
12. Your employees request that customers call them back when the employees aren't so busy. (Customers should never be told to call back. Request the customer's number instead.)
13. Your employees rush through calls, forcing customers off the phone at the earliest opportunity. (Be a little more discreet.

Politely suggest that you've got the information you need and you must move on to other calls.)

14. Your employees obnoxiously bellow, 'What's this in reference to?' effectively humbling customers and belittling their requests. (Screening techniques can be used with a little more warmth and finesse. If a caller has mistakenly come your way, do your best to point him or her in the right direction.)

15. Your employees freely admit to customers that they hate their jobs. (This simply makes the entire company look bad. And don't think such a moment of candour or lapse in judgement won't get back to the boss.)

In defence of customer service workers, customers can be rude too. And customer service jobs can often be thankless, with little motivation or incentive to do the job right. But the problem here is that life for customer service employees may not be fair. Customers can be rude and get away with it. Employees cannot – if they want to help their companies to succeed and keep their jobs as well.

■ Don't use conversational 'brand barriers' that send the message to the customer that he or she is not important, you don't have time for them, or they are somehow inferior to you or your way of thinking. Here are some typical barriers that customers encounter every day when dealing with companies:

  – *Contradicting the customer.* Sometimes the company representative will argue with the customer over points that are irrelevant to the main issue. (In face-to-face meetings the arguing is usually accompanied by extreme facial and body language actions, such as raising eyebrows, rolling the eyes, throwing the head back, or turning to look in another direction. And yes, I'm talking about the company representative, not the customer!)

  – *Belittling or discounting the customer's concerns.* This comes across as a complete put-down, implying that the company representative has superior knowledge. When dealing with highly complex or technical issues, business staff may well have a greater degree of understanding. However, the customer is there to be served, not sentenced.

- *Labelling or stereotyping the customer*. Even in the 21st century it's not at all uncommon for sexist, racial or political undertones to exist in a conversation with a client. Implications of the customer being less able in whatever matter because of a label applied to them is a definite 'no-no' under any circumstances.

- *Prejudging the customer's motive*. When a product or service complaint is received, it is very easy to blame the customer, or impute a motive of dishonesty as to why the product is being returned, or a refund is being requested. Yes, there are unscrupulous people around, but suggesting that one of your customers belongs in that category will never help set the right image for your brand. Even if your gut feel tells you that you are being deceived, if you don't have absolute proof, always give the benefit of the doubt.

■ **Don't use a digitally created, generic robot voice on your automated telephone system, if you have one.** Apart from the fact that it sounds the same as your competitors' – as if that isn't cause enough for concern – it immediately sends the message to your customers that they are not important enough to be addressed by a human being. (Remember that perception is reality.) Use a human voice, and one that is specifically matched to your company's overall image. If your system is split, with an automatic set-up but with your staff answering at various times or in other offices, how are their voices aligned with the automated voice? Do they use the same greeting as the virtual one? Do they use the same vocabulary, the same type of sentence make-up when giving out information to the customer? Again, ensure that your Brand Lexicon is utilised at all times throughout this process.

■ **Do ensure that your voicemail service is up to date and helpful.** Does it currently churn out typical (and boring) message like, 'I'm away from my desk right now...'? Of course you're away from your desk, or you'd answer the call, wouldn't you? Worse still is a message that gives alternatives as to where you might be, such as, 'I'm either in a meeting or on another call.' So, what is this? A guessing game? Actually, I don't much care where you are. If I can't speak to you, then simply confirm I've reached the right person and let me leave a message – or let me know what alternatives there might be, like contacting a colleague of yours (as long as you don't have to send me all the way back to the switchboard to do it).

And never be like those seemingly absent-minded staff members who leave a message on their voicemail stating that they'll be back in the office on a particular day, then when you call four days later, the same message is on their voicemail – and you still can't get hold of them. If employees can't even remember to update their own voicemail, how can I, as a customer, trust them to look after my business?

Putting your brand on the right track

Dum. De de da dum. That's my written rendition of the catchy little three-second, five-note Intel jingle that we all know... and maybe some even love. It started life as part of Intel's 'Intel Inside®' campaign, which kicked off way back in 1991 and is now one of the most globally recognised 'audio logos', sitting up there with the Nokia ringtone as well as Windows and Apple start-up sounds.

Those who think that sensory perception influence doesn't work for things like technology products need to think again. The way Intel has been able to take a highly complex computer processing chip and market it to the general public (who are ignorant for the most part as to what it does or how it does it) as a 'must-have' in their PCs has been described as one of the most brilliant marketing strategies in the past decade. In 2005 the Intel brand was worth an estimated $35.6 billion and ranked among the top five in the world. And you can bet that the little ditty had a lot to do with its success.

We've always been aware that music is one of the greatest generators of emotion. The silent movies of yesteryear would have been less entertaining without the piano player sitting in the cinema and playing music to match the scenes. Even the movies of today, with their ultra-special video effects, are pretty bland without the opening soundtrack and all the incidental music that accompanies it. Music can stir us, motivate us, make us happy, sad, angry or ecstatic – and sometimes just a few short notes are all it takes. Dr Adrian North and Dr David Hargreaves, researchers at Leicester University, have suggested that brands with appropriate music are 96 per cent more likely to be recalled than those with no music at all.

You're probably familiar with the experiment by Pavlov, who in the 1900s rang a bell when dogs in his laboratory were fed, thus associating their feeding time with the ringing of a bell. After a while, as soon as the dogs heard the sound of the bell they responded by salivating. Before Pavlov introduced the bell, they had salivated only when they actually had the food in front of them. This 'classical conditioning', as it became known, applies to people, too. Just think about when you were at school and the bell rang, either at the end of a lesson or at lunchtime, and how this became a strong sensory cue.

Sound actually requires less concentration than the visual sense. Music playing in the background isn't something we have to focus on, yet it can enhance our activity. Eating at a restaurant is a typical example of where music can add to the perception of the whole culinary experience, but sadly this is often one of a very limited number of uses of music to evoke emotions. This needs to change. The digital revolution has created a whole new opportunity for music to take its place as a significant sensory influence, and one that is affordable for even the smallest business.

Today, there is an abundance of suppliers offering royalty-free sounds, music loops and jingles that can be purchased for less than the cost of a restaurant meal, and if your budget can stretch that far, you can have a full-length 'corporate' song penned exclusively for your business and downloaded as an MP3 file straight to your desktop – and the desktops of your customers, too. Gone are the days when music used in a business environment was limited to a worn-out cassette tape or eight-track playing repeatedly – and often annoyingly – in the background of some retail store, or the elevator music that attempted to calm people as they made their way to the 30th floor, or (for those of us in the United Kingdom who remember that far back) the chimes of 'Greensleeves' that signalled the arrival of the ice-cream van in the street outside your house.

Not all businesses are able to incorporate each of the five senses into every single business activity. However, that doesn't mean you shouldn't try! With a little creativity you should be able to come up with several ways in which music can be used to your advantage. In fact, there are three main areas where music can be used to improve a customer's brand experience:

- audio logos and jingles;
- customer guidance;
- spatial enhancement.

They make up what I call your Brand Soundtrack™. Let's consider the three musical areas in a little more detail.

Audio logos and jingles

An audio logo can be used in just about every part of your business where your customer (or even your supplier) is making contact with you. Your website, for example, is an obvious place where music can be a significant enhancement. Whether your musical ditty is a full-length piece of music or a short, snappy jingle, music can deepen recall, so that it is more likely to take its place in long-term memory.

Your website can include your audio logo or jingle as an opening device – like the www.newstoday.com website, for example. (You won't forget your visit there, yet the jingle is less than a few seconds long.) Or it could include a whole music track that you can offer to your customers as a downloadable MP3 file.

Starbucks' *Hear Music* CD compilations, on sale to its customers in its coffee stores and online, were not only a way to enhance the Starbucks brand by offering customers the opportunity to experience all different kinds of music (and winning Grammy awards in the process) but provided an additional lucrative revenue stream. In 2007 the *Hear Music* catalogue was put on iTunes, including specially created playlists. How's that for maximising the use of your Brand Soundtrack™? Of course, if you are going the 'full track' route it is important that you know your customers' musical taste. Bad selections of music can do damage to any brand, like a poor choice in any aspect of the sensory spectrum.

Also, if you do plan to introduce music to your website in excess of just an opening audio logo, give visitors the chance to turn the sound off. It isn't that they might not be in the mood to listen to your heavy rock track or the specially written orchestral work, but they could be accessing your site from their workplace or other environment where loud music would not be welcome.

Blow your trumpet, sound your horn

Whether jingle or entire song, music is not limited to the web. What about including a CD of your music or a copy of your logo or jingle in your promotional items, your public relations press kit, or as an introduction at the start of your business presentations and included in the handouts you make available?

But isn't specially composed music way beyond the budget of a small business or non-profit organisation? It needn't be. As with your visual logo, there are many students and aspiring musicians out there who would relish the opportunity to compose a jingle or perform a piece of music that would be heard by all your customers; who knows what further work they might obtain as a result?

Some years ago, before the digital age came upon us, I recruited a local amateur band to compose and perform a song for a boat manufacturer, with a very small fee as a reward. The resultant song was copied to cassette tape for promotional giveaways and used in the company's radio advertising as well as at all its exhibitions and events. Not only was the song a huge success in helping to create a memorable brand for the business but other suppliers to the boat company wanted a similar recording.

The band also received a number of bookings to play at private events and a link-up with one of their stage shows and the boat manufacturer succeeded in obtaining significant sales. Backed up by public relations and media exposure, the whole approach ran for over three years, during which time thousands of copies of the song were given away to customers.

The boat manufacturer, which employed only six people, gained a brand reputation way beyond its size of operation, compared to other manufacturers that were spending considerable sums of money on purely visual approaches to their branding.

An audio logo can be sung, played or digitally created. Apart from the obvious point that it needs to be memorable, it needs to be carefully selected to be relevant to your brand and your customer base. If your product or service is state-of-the-art, you may need some rousing, motivational sonic logo or music as part of the customer experience. On the other hand, products and services that promote calm or tranquillity would probably need something softer and gentler. Relevancy is not just limited to the actual tune.

Whatever lyrics are involved and whatever genre or style of music you have selected, it must align with the rest of your brand's ideals and values if it's to be a successful part of the customer experience. If you operate a business or organisation involved in fair trade, animal welfare or not-for-profit activities, then your singer or composer shouldn't be known as someone who flouts or opposes the values you and your customers hold. The bottom line is: what do the customers relate to? Researchers North and Hargreaves, mentioned earlier, contend that customers are much more likely to buy a product when they like – and relate to – the brand's music, compared to when the music doesn't fit their preferences, or they actually find the music annoying. It may seem an obvious point, but it's one that is often disregarded, especially in the retail sector. Choose your music wisely and your brand will reap the rewards.

Good telephone etiquette

When customers interface with your business, they need to know where to go and what to do in order to satisfy their enquiry or obtain information. The rise of call centres and interactive voice response (IVR) has meant that the first few minutes of customers calling a business are taken up in pushing buttons and making choices, with the intention of making it easier and faster for them to get to the source they need.

Unfortunately, owing to the way such technology is poorly managed and ill-conceived, customers are often less than enamoured by call waiting queues extending beyond reasonable times, turgid music they cannot turn off, or difficulty in plotting their course through all the alternative telephone menus. What's left of the customer experience is not so much a shining example of the firm's brand, but rather a lesson in how not to do it. Can you improve the caller's experience in your business? Consider how music might bring some positive branding to the table.

Whatever type of telephone system you have, its audio content is part of your brand, from the initial greeting to the on-hold music. The question is, are you maximising the opportunities to present the right sounds to the caller? Consider these two main telephone points:

- When your customers ring your business number, what do they hear? How about creating an audio logo and using this as an element of the greeting part of your message?

- What about your 'on-hold' situation? What do customers hear – silence? That's the worst option of them all, as the customer doesn't know whether he or she is still on hold or has actually been disconnected.

Poor telephone performance on behalf of a business is one of the main reasons why customers hang up their phone after a short while. Statistics show that up to 60 per cent of callers will put their phone down if faced with silence while on hold for more than 30 seconds, and a third of those won't call back. Who can blame them?

Other companies utilise a feed from a radio station to provide music. This is marginally better, but do you really want your customers listening to the radio advertisements about someone else's products or services? You could, of course, provide information about new products or services while they are waiting. It's estimated that 20 per cent of people make a purchase or a purchasing decision based on the information they hear while on hold. However, some psychologists suggest that providing sales information while a caller is on hold only creates confusion in the person's mind, because this new information diverts their attention away from the original reason for their call.

Whether you choose this route and have music in the background to the voiceover person, or play music on its own, the key point is to ensure that the music is relevant to your brand and your customers. Do callers to your company have a choice of what to listen to? Is it their kind of music – or yours? What images do you want your callers to have while they are on hold? How can you align the vision and sound aspects of your brand at this contact point? Audio logos and music can also be used successfully in voicemail and enhance any instructions on leaving a message, as well as providing another audio sensory cue about your brand.

Giving customers audio guidance

Navigation is a very important aspect of customer contact, whether it be on the telephone or on your website. Studies show that when organisations rely on speech-guided telephone options only, the numerous menu choices can often overload short-term memory.

Here's where earcons – short one- or two-note tones – can be used to enhance the customer's ability to navigate menu options. (Earcons are to the sound sense what graphic icons are to the visual sense.) Each menu option could have a corresponding earcon, but if certain menu paths were known to be used frequently, the earcons could be composed of notes that when pressed in a certain sequence made a recognisable tune that the caller could remember.

If that sounds a little over the top, consider how just five simple tones in Spielberg's 1977 movie classic *Close Encounters of the Third Kind* prompted anyone with a musical instrument to learn how to play them. Even some thirty years down the line, those notes still linger in the memories today of those old enough to remember the film.

Earcons work well on website menus, too. Each menu item could have a separate earcon associated with it that played when the desired menu option was selected. Research has shown that website menus using tones that increase in pitch as users move down the options or across the navigation bar make the task of finding the right place in which to gather the required information a faster, simpler and more enjoyable activity. What's more, while the advent of CSS coding for websites has made accessibility for blind and partially sighted computer users easier, auditory options vastly increase their ability to interact with computer navigation.

Finally, why not consider using earcons as part of your business presentations? Each bullet point on your slides could appear with an accompanying sound – something that most presentation software includes in the animation part of the programme, but often gets left out. With appropriate background music to lead towards your introduction, you can fire off your presentation with an audio logo appearing at the beginning of your talk (along with the visual version, of course), and utilise earcons throughout the salient points of your presentation to guide the audience sonically as well as visually.

Your final slide could be accompanied by music from your Brand Soundtrack™ as you voice-over your closing remarks, culminating in the audio and visual logos being presented as the final sensory cue. Do this, and you should be streets ahead of the usual boring, wooden performance many presenters inflict on their audiences.

Spatial enhancement

Wherever your customers meet your business in a setting, whether it's a store, reception area or office, the spatial aspects of the environment cannot be discounted. Customers will either hear what you want them to hear – and what is appropriate at that time – or they'll hear the 'default' sounds.

Depending on the place in question, these sounds could range from badly selected music tracks playing too loudly for comfort (or too silently to be worth the effort) to the cacophony of noise generated by machinery, multiple conversations and telephones ringing.

Spatial considerations are just as important as the other parts of your Brand Soundtrack™ if you want to improve the customer experience using the sound sense. It is also essential for your staff to be able to work in spatial settings where sound has been planned, rather than left to chance. In fact, studies suggest that noisy workplaces are the primary cause of poor productivity levels, causing reductions in efficiency of almost two-thirds when compared to a noise-free environment.

Continual noise is going to cause stress, which in turn will create job dissatisfaction – and this will have an automatically detrimental effect on your brand. You may not want music playing in the office area, but there are many companies out there offering low-cost ways to cut down noise, including acoustic room dividers, sound-absorbing partitions between desks, noise-absorbing carpeting and soundproofing tiles on walls and ceilings. If you own a factory, don't leave out employees here, either. It's likely that health and safety regulations will determine minimum requirements, but why not enhance the workplace with appropriate noise-reduction materials and get the benefit of a more productive workforce?

Perhaps one of the biggest problem areas for utilising appropriate sound is the retail environment. For instance, go into a retail store or a not-for-profit shop and you'll usually hear background music that is meant to improve the spatial setting. All too often, however, what really happens is that customers (and employees) listen to the same old CD tracks (sometimes chosen by the staff with little or no guidance, and often breaching copyright or public performance issues) playing day after day, with the notion that any kind of music is better than nothing at all.

How wrong! Music, like all sensory content, is highly subjective, and without a full appreciation of what kind of music the main bulk of your customers prefer, and how it fits with your overall brand image, it might be more of an irritant than a customer experience enhancer.

Don't play it again, Sam: the worst in-store anthems

British retail workers are being driven to distraction by the songs that provide the soundtrack to their working lives, according to research conducted by RetailChoice.com in July 2005. Three-quarters of shop staff admitted to being irritated by in-store music.

A staggering 31 per cent of shop workers have to endure the same album between 6 and 20 times a week, with 16 per cent hearing the same record more than 20 times during the course of a week.

Those working in the fashion and footwear retail sectors suffer the most from 'repetitive record syndrome'. The most overplayed records on the high street come courtesy of:

1. Britney Spears
2. Usher
3. Kylie Minogue
4. 50 Cent
5. Robbie Williams
6. Akon
7. Beyoncé
8. Blue
=9. Justin Timberlake
=9. Michael Jackson

And it's not just the staff whose nerves are being tested. Forty per cent of shop workers receive complaints from customers about the maddening music played as they part with their hard-earned cash.

Christmas is the most testing time for the ears of the nation's retail workers. *Jingle Bells* tops the list of the most hated seasonal songs, with Slade's *Merry Christmas Everyone* and *White Christmas* by Bing Crosby also annoying retail staff.

Overall, pop music is still top of the shops' play list, with the majority of stores opting for this genre. Forty-two per cent of those polled believe that pop music in shops actually encourages shoppers to buy more. However, when it comes to motivating shoppers to part with their cash, reggae music fares the worst. Just 5 per cent of shop staff notice an increase in spending when reggae is playing.

Greg Baines, marketing manager for RetailChoice.com, commented:

> Music is an essential part of the retail experience, and can help to make or break the ambience for both staff and customers. In the words of Britney Spears, music can be Toxic to the shopping process if stores aren't careful. We would recommend that retailers who overplay records from our shop flop list should think again and consult employees to achieve a varied playlist that is well received by both shoppers and staff.

© *RetailChoice.com. Reproduced by kind permission.*

Main considerations for choice of background music should therefore include:

- Factors such as the customers' age groups, ethnic background, familiarity with the music and personal tastes regarding the musical genres being played (eg popular, country, jazz, western or classical). Popular music itself has sub-genres that will appeal only to selected audiences (for example, those with a nostalgic liking for old 1950s or 1960s hits). A fashion boutique serving teenagers is unlikely to play background music equally suitable for a dentist's surgery or financial planning centre. If you have a wide spectrum of different types of customer, the key, as always, is to appeal to your core group of best customers and use them as the model for your sensory focus.
- Quality considerations, including the clarity of the music system, the room acoustics and the corresponding volume in the store. Shoppers will not appreciate having to listen to distorted music, or the need to stand in one corner of the store in order to hear the faint sound coming from a single loudspeaker. Volume levels will need to be varied according to the type of business you operate. Studies have shown that while music may be a positive store enhancement, when complex tasks need to be performed, or where concentration is needed, music can detract

from rather than reinforce your brand. Plan your music accordingly.

- Time-of-day options relative to types of customer. Should songs played after, say, 6 pm be of the same genre as music used during the daytime? This will depend on whether or not your customer profiles change throughout the day. For example, some restaurants or cafés will serve a younger set of consumers during the day compared to those in the evening, in which case the music selection will need to be significantly different.

- Employees working in the store, especially on the tills. *Men's Health* magazine (April 1996) claimed that when an employee liked the background music, performance and productivity could improve by as much as 10 per cent. Customers' preferences must come first. But here is where the proper staff recruitment approaches are essential (see Chapter 16). If the staff are fully aligned with your brand values and ideals, their musical tastes shouldn't be a million miles away from what your customers like.

- Consider alternatives to non-stop music tracks, such as piping in a relevant radio station. The downside of this is the matter of control – over both what the DJ is saying and what products and services are being advertised that might compete with your own. Of course, with a larger budget you could create your own in-store radio station, using music attuned to the customer and interspersed with store announce-ments relevant to the shopping experience. According to some studies conducted, more than 40 per cent of shoppers who recall hearing an in-store audio advertisement make purchases they weren't planning.

Chosen correctly, then, music can have a significant effect on sales as well as your overall brand experience. In 1982 a study in the United States by researcher Ronald Milliman showed that when a chain of supermarkets played slow background music, shoppers were encouraged to stay longer and spend more on products. Milliman went on to check out background music in restaurants, discovering that those listening to slow music ate at a more leisurely pace and bought nearly 50 per cent more alcoholic drinks.

Other restaurant studies of piped music have shown that classical music can increase the purchase of more expensive wines, because of the music's association with quality. Country-specific associations work well, too. In 1999, North, Hargreaves and McKendrick conducted a 'wine-aisle' experiment that consisted of playing German and French music on alternate days over a period of two weeks in a supermarket that sold a selection of European wines.

The results showed that French wine outsold German wine by 3:1 when the background music was French. When German music was played, German wine outsold French wine 2:1.

Music while you work

Of course, if you don't operate retail environments, none of the above will apply directly. But what about your offices – and in particular your reception area? Even if you meet very few customers face to face, your reception area can still be an important feature of your brand for those who do visit your premises.

What does your reception area sound like? The chances are, the only sounds emanating from its quarters are the receptionist answering the phone, or the sound of the entrance door swinging open and shut. By having music playing softly in your reception area you can create a soothing environment for your visitors. This can be particularly effective if they have arrived stressed because of a problematic journey, or inclement weather.

Your audio logo can also help create consistency in your branding efforts. Perhaps the audio logo could sound whenever the door is opened by the arriving visitors. Or, if you have so many customers coming to see you that it would become annoying, you might decide to use it sparingly when a particular activity occurs – for example, when the clock reaches every 15-minute interval. Obviously, no sound should be so loud or repetitive that it defeats the object. But used carefully, at the right time and volume level, your audio logo or any other music can create a sonic branding that will add real depth to the customer experience.

If you provide medical, dental or other healthcare services, music in your reception or waiting room area is as important as the visual aspects, if not more so. Patients can become less anxious if soft, calming music is playing in the background. Studies show that friends or family accompanying those undergoing treatment can also become less stressed by listening to the same music. Other research carried out suggests that some types of music even help to lower blood pressure. But beware: the wrong type can actually raise it. What most studies seem to indicate is that best results derive from people being able to listen to the music of their choice, rather than being given music that the practice thinks is soothing. Once again, the key is to find out what the clients or patients prefer. One possible suggestion is to let them bring their own music and provide headsets, much like those on aircraft. For your particular practice this might be going too far. But you'll never know unless you ask.

Ultimately, wherever and however you use audio, the key to its effectiveness will once again come down to consistency, plus the exclusivity of the sounds. Even large organisations have often created a memorable, personalised piece of music, or a short, catchy tune or jingle, but have restricted its use to, for example, an advertising campaign on radio or television.

Once the campaign has finished its course, or another advertising agency is appointed with a different creative approach, the music is dropped, only to be replaced by another piece of music totally different from the one people had become familiar with. Limiting your music to an isolated part of your customer experience does little good for your brand. Granted, there may be times when you don't want to use sounds (if you have a dedicated complaints line, it's not going to be the best idea to start the conversation off with a burst of energetic music, or a snappy-happy jingle), but in the main, repetition of your sound brand will be an essential part of your desire to create an outstanding customer experience.

Don't miss audio opportunities

I remember in 2006 when the German manufacturer Kärcher created a television advertisement for its VC 6300 vacuum cleaner. The ad featured a song called *Sweetest Eyes* by Marjolein. Within weeks of its being aired, the internet was flooded with enquiries (including several from me) as to where the song could be obtained. Kärcher made it available as a free MP3 download on its main German website, much to the delight of those who liked the song.

Just a short while later, I attended an outdoor event where Kärcher had its various products on display, including the VC 6300. However, there wasn't a single reference to the song in the advert, not even the faintest whisper of the soundtrack. I'm not sure whether Kärcher even realised the impact it had had in the United Kingdom. There were so many aspects of the brand that could have benefited from the song's popularity. Not only could the salespeople have played it in their demonstration, but they could have given copies away, along with product information.

If they were planning to penetrate the UK market for cleaning equipment, they might just have thought about bringing Marjolein over for the event, or had some publicity shots taken to accompany the song. Kärcher could have begun a strategy to get its brand into my long-term memory. Now, so much further down the line, I didn't even think of Kärcher when I purchased a new cleaner.

Some companies get it right. Over a 20-year period, British Airways used a piece of music called *Flower Duet* by Léo Delibes in its television commercials. The music proved very popular with viewers – to the point that when it was first discarded, so many people protested that BA brought it back. Not only that, but BA exploited this sensory awareness by playing the music in passenger lounges as well as piping it through BA planes before take-off. Premier-class passengers were given free copies of the classical CD that contained their soundtrack.

Surveys have shown that the music has remained firmly associated with the airline, despite Ford adopting the same piece in 1999 for its Galaxy model advertisements. So popular is the music that when BA fired its advertising agency of 23 years, M & C Saatchi, and gave the business to Bartle Bogle Hegarty, the music was still retained for its Executive Club flyer programme. Now that's what I call having your brand on track.

The sweet smell of brand success

Forgive the pun, but when it comes to enhancing a brand, using aromas and fragrances is not something to be sniffed at. Our sense of smell is often taken for granted, yet it's one of the most powerful senses we possess. According to Martin Lindstrom in his highly influential book *Brand Sense* (2005), research conducted by Millward Brown on Lindstrom's behalf suggested that as much as 75 per cent of our emotions are generated by what we smell. This may be due to the fact that of the five senses, only our sense of smell has a direct link to the limbic lobe of the brain, the area we know as the 'emotional control centre', which contains, among other things, the amygdala, which we discussed earlier.

Although each one of us has a personal preference when it comes to certain smells, there are enough generalisations about smell preference to create specific scents for a positive customer experience. For example, vanilla has been a popular aroma for many years. I remember reading super-salesman Tom Hopkins' book *How to Master the Art of Selling* (1983), which talked about real estate salespeople baking a few drops of vanilla in the oven in order to evoke images of warmth, shelter and home cooking for potential buyers. Perfume counters in departmental stores have a natural outlet by default for all kinds of fragrances. And restaurants, coffee bars and bistros obviously rely on enticing customers through their doors by creating smells of delicious foods and beverages, which not only trigger the emotions but put the salivary glands into overdrive.

Smells evoke memories

One of the key benefits of the sense of smell is its ability to recall past memories in which the same scent was experienced. While our other senses such as sight, sound and touch can also bring back previous events, the memories evoked by our sense of smell tend to be deeper and more intense, thus creating stronger emotions. In fact, there is much evidence to show that people can recall smells with 65 per cent accuracy even after 12 months or so. This compares very favourably with our visual recall ability, which drops to around 50 per cent after only 3 months.

One of the best examples of smell-sense recollection comes from the 'madeleine passage' written by 20th-century novelist Marcel Proust. In fact, his narrative has led to many studies into what psychologists have called 'Proustian memory' (or, as Proust called it, 'involuntary memory'). This refers to the times where an aroma or fragrance being experienced in the present can recall a past memory in great detail and evoke an emotional response as a result – usually the same emotions involved in that first encounter – without the person consciously thinking about it.

The madeleine passage appears in Proust's classic seven-volume work *Remembrance of Things Past* in one of the collection's novels, *Swann's Way*. After dipping a French madeleine cake (a small shell-shaped pastry) into some lime-blossom tea, the fragrance and subsequent taste bring back childhood memories – several hundred pages of them. Writing as the narrator Charles Swann, Proust says:

> ... and as soon as I had recognised the taste of madeleine soaked in her decoction of lime-blossom which my aunt used to give me... immediately the old grey house upon the street, where her room was, rose up like a stage set... and with the house the town, from morning to night and in all weathers, the Square where I used to be sent before lunch, the streets along which I used to run errands, the country roads we took when it was fine.

Despite the obvious potential of incorporating aromas into the customer experience, many companies – even blue-chip corporations – have been slow to exploit this powerful sensory stimulator. Alex Moskvin, Vice President of BrandEmotions™, the internal brand development agency of global flavour and aroma experts International Flavors and Fragrances Inc (IFF), states, 'Brand owners are becoming more aware of the importance of scent in sensory branding. Of all the senses, the sense of smell is "hard-wired" to the emotional centres of the brain. Scent is the new – and last – frontier of emotional branding.' IFF has already worked with Samsung to create a scent for Samsung Experience Stores, and created, then bottled, the smell of a new sneaker for athletic shoe retailer Foot Locker. The scent was used for in-store sampling and as part of its print and outdoor advertising campaign throughout Europe.

A handful of other businesses have also been willing to experiment with smells and aromas, with excellent results. In the United Kingdom, for example, high street retailer W H Smith has used pine fragrance at Christmas time to enhance its in-store festive decoration – a simple (and perhaps obvious) addition, yet highly effective. London shirtmaker Thomas Pink is said to pump the smell of air-dried linen into its shops, while travel agent Thomson Holidays has scented its shops with the smell of coconut, evoking thoughts of tropical settings in the minds of potential holidaymakers. Other applications include some car manufacturers spraying the interiors of their vehicles with a 'new car' smell (although Rolls-Royce was doing that back in the 1960s). General Motors created a scent (known as Nuance) for the leather seats inside its Cadillacs, and Toyota's Hybrid X cars feature an automatic misting of in-car scents. In 2007, Kumho Tires in the United States introduced the ECSTA DX range of 'aroma tyres' impregnated with lavender scents and announced plans to expand the range to incorporate orange and jasmine scents.

Hotel chains have also begun to utilise the sense of smell to greet customers as they enter the lobby. In the Omni Hotel in Los Angeles the scent of lemongrass and green tea is used at a low level to make guests feel relaxed and comfortable in preparation for their stay, while Langham Hotels has globally adopted ginger flower as the brand's aroma. Westin Hotels introduced its trademark White Tea scent by featuring it in a print advertisement campaign that included a scented strip embedded with the fragrance. The distinctive White Tea smell in its hotels prompted hundreds of requests from guests for samples of the aroma, and a range of 'White Tea by Westin™' products, including candles, pot-pourri and room oil diffusers, has been launched to capitalise on the customer demand.

In 2001 the world's most advanced giant animatronic dinosaur was unveiled at the Tyrannosaurus Rex exhibition in London's Natural History Museum. In order to make the exhibition a full sensory experience, the museum commissioned UK aroma specialists Dale Air to capture the authentic smell of the fearsome beast. The brief was to simulate the smell of the animal drenched in the blood of its prey, reeking of rotten meat and scarred with infected wounds – and have this acrid smell released every time the creature opened its mouth.

In order to eliminate guesswork on exactly the kind of smell that would be encountered, Dale Air consulted Dr Angela O'Connell, the museum's Head of Vertebrate Palaeontology, to determine specifics relating to the dinosaur's breath. However, the resultant odour was so authentic that the museum felt it would be too sickly for the public to withstand. As an alternative, the company created the smell of the environment that the creature occupied – a boggy, swampy-type smell that incorporated just a slight hint of the creature's breath.

Some companies have dabbled with the use of aromas as part of specific time-limited promotions. In 2005, JCB, the largest credit card issuer in Japan, launched the JCB LINDA Sweet Card, which featured a citrus-based fragrance combining the smells of mandarin, grapefruit and lemon. According to JCB, an internet survey of over 6,000 of its cardholders highlighted the fact that fragrances played an important part in their lives.

The Singapore Girl sensory brand

Perhaps one of the best examples of using the sense of smell to gain greater brand perception has been that of Singapore Airlines. In 1968 the airline created what was to become a globally recognised symbol of true in-flight customer care through its 'Singapore Girl' image. Its female cabin crew were chosen for their beautiful looks and were given in-depth training on how to talk to passengers, how to serve food and even how to walk up and down the aeroplane dressed in their sarong kebaya uniforms designed by French fashion house Pierre Balmain. The whole customer experience utilised sound, touch, taste and sight.

Then, in the early 1990s, Singapore Airlines completed the entire five-senses sensory platform by creating Stefan Floridian Waters, a specially formulated scent used for the perfume of the cabin crew and sprayed on to the hot face towels given to their passengers before take-off. Regular customers could easily identify with this trademarked fragrance as soon as they boarded the aircraft, thus prompting emotions of reassurance and being on 'familiar territory', while new customers would automatically differentiate the airline through its distinctive smell even before sampling the rest of the sensory experience.

When, in 2007, a review of the Singapore Girl approach was conducted amid criticisms of outdated sexist imagery that promoted the idea of subservient Oriental women, the sensory experience was never called into question. Perhaps that's not surprising when you consider that by involving all the sensory experiences, including distinctive smells, Singapore Airlines' customer experience has led to a string of awards, including the Business Traveller USA 2007 award for Best Overall Airline in the World for the 16th consecutive year, and the 'World's Best Cabin Crew Service' by the Business Traveller Asia-Pacific Awards in 2006 for 17 years running.

Defining your brand's smell

Of course, the above examples of the use of the smell sense are from large corporations. But they serve to show that, with some applied creativity, fragrances and perfumes really can enhance the brand. How, then, can your company or non-profit operation reap the benefits of using the sense of smell? The answer is by creating a BrandScent – a bouquet that is used by you frequently and consistently. That doesn't have to mean spending huge amounts of money on a special formula that no one else in the world can have. Rather, it means that matching an 'off-the-shelf' scent to the emotions you want to create, then being consistent with its use, will automatically give your brand an extra dimension that it didn't have before.

Matching your brand emotions to the right scent is obviously of paramount importance. Generally speaking, aromas will fall into two main categories: those with calming, relaxing qualities, and those that stimulate and energise. Table 10.1 gives a list of some of the common aromas for creating a particular mood.

Table 10.1 Moods created by particular scents

Scent	Mood
vanilla	relaxed, soothed
orange	purifying and refreshing
cinnamon	stimulating and refreshing
peppermint	energising
pine	stimulating
rose	calming
eucalyptus	stimulating
lemon	stimulating and refreshing
lavender	calming and soothing

Scents can basically be utilised in three main areas of business: the environment, the product or service itself and promotional activity.

Your BrandScent environment

If you operate a business where customers meet on your premises, establishing a BrandScent for your reception is one of the most differentiating actions you can take. After all, what does a reception area or meeting room usually smell like? Often, nothing at all! By giving your main customer meeting points a particular scent that they can associate with, you're replicating the advantage that the Singapore Airlines' scent strategy has created for that company.

Using, for example, a lavender or rose fragrance in a subtle manner can not only create a memorable emotional cue but also calm down customers who might arrive stressed or angry at someone or something they might have experienced on the way to see you – in which case they'll thank you for providing something of a solace from the hassle! I'm taking it for granted that whether your customer toilets are located in the reception area or elsewhere, the smell they give off is always pleasant. Many people – myself included – judge the standards of a company by the state of its toilet and washroom facilities. After all, if you can't even be bothered to ensure that the smell of cleanliness and hygiene pervades this area, how can I be confident about your concern over any other aspect of business?

For sales areas and showrooms, whether they are an extension of a factory unit or within a retail environment, using scent can directly help boost sales. Casino operators in the United States discovered that scenting the area around slot machines with a particular aroma could generate as much as a 45 per cent increase in business. And Dr Alan Hirsch, the founder and neurological director of the Smell and Taste Treatment and Research Foundation in Chicago, did a study that showed consumers would be willing to pay $10 more for shoes in a floral-scented environment than exactly the same shoes in an unscented environment.

These results reflect the findings of an experiment conducted by Martin Lindstrom, again in his book *Brand Sense* (2005). A pair of Nike shoes was placed in each of two rooms, with one pair having a faint smell sprayed into the shoes – so faint, in fact, that people couldn't even smell it. In 84 per cent of the cases the respondents stated a preference for the Nike shoes with the smell, even though they couldn't explain their reasoning. They also confirmed that they'd be willing to pay more than $10 extra for these shoes.

One holiday company in the United Kingdom offers the chance for customers to experience a virtual tour of its holiday destinations through the use of a 3D headset and accompanying aromas. For instance, a trip to Egypt would incorporate the smell of herbs and spices at an open-air market as the would-be holidaymaker is seeing the sights and hearing the sounds of the virtual tour. Other scenes take in the musty smells of a pharaoh's tomb, a refreshing sea breeze and the fragrance of coconut suntan oil by the swimming pool.

Exhibition stands are also an obvious place where an essence can gain the attention of those passing by. Small diffusers, electronic units or even a simple aerosol spray can be used with ease to add that extra sense to an otherwise bland stand. If nothing else, a pleasant aroma can help mask the undesirable smell of body odour emanating from staff who've probably had to arrive early, get in a sweat setting up the stand and then remain *in situ* for several hours, often with few breaks.

Charity shops – a smelly problem?

Talking of unpleasant smells, many not-for-profit organisations in the United Kingdom run high street charity shops (often called 'thrift shops' in the United States) as a means of generating extra income. There is usually one main problem with most of them: their aroma is very bad. This is because the shops are staffed by overworked volunteers who receive bundles of clothes donated by the public every day. Most of the time the items of clothing handed in have not been washed or have been stored for a long period of time before they are given to the charity. With so many piles of such clothing in the back room to be sorted out, the whole shop develops an aroma that, in my experience, sits somewhere between out-and-out body odour and the fusty smell of a damp and derelict building.

The solution would only require the application of a regular spray to eliminate the bad odours – and if the charity ran a string of shops, using the same scent in each one would also differentiate them from other charities' retail operations. I once worked with a small non-profit organisation that ran six shops all suffering from BBO (Bad Brand Odour). By utilising a combination of orange and pine scent (which could even be noticed by passers-by on the pavement), along with the incorporation of the other major sensory elements, the shops all increased their in-store traffic by over 40 per cent in just two weeks. What's more, the special fragrance was mixed at no cost, on the basis of a bulk purchase by the charity. Even the diffusers were lent free of charge.

I've found it personally disappointing that some charity fundraisers who have heard my presentations on this powerful sensory approach have responded negatively by stating, 'We've better things to do with our time and money than wonder what our organisation smells like.' Well, everyone's entitled to an opinion. But when it comes to the facts about how the human brain works, the evidence for sensory branding is there for all to see – and smell. Used in the right manner, scent branding can boost sales by a surprising amount – and there really is no better emotion-evoking associative power with which to influence the customer of today.

Scenting the product or service

In many small businesses, when I've suggested considering ways in which the company's product or service could be enhanced by fragrance, the executives often sit scratching their heads and, by not thinking 'outside the box', reject the idea of branding through smell as unworkable – especially if they make something that, according to them, is a product that's unsuitable for such improvement. In reality, there are very few products and services that cannot be given an aromatic makeover in some way or form.

I state quite emphatically in my brand workshops that almost any business can utilise the sense of smell as a way to improve its product or service. As a challenge to any sceptics, I once went through an entire *Yellow Pages* directory to see what companies were ruled out of scent branding. The first category heading was for abattoirs – notorious for complaints from the people living nearby about the smell of waste. But by carrying out a quick search on the internet, I discovered numerous companies manufacturing scents and enzyme-based ingredients to eliminate slaughterhouse odours and improve the smell.

Many of the *Yellow Pages* headings that followed provided obvious opportunities, from flower shops (if you can't create a signature smell for a business that sells flowers, you ought to sell up tomorrow – better yet, this afternoon) to iron and steel merchants, from laundry services to musical instrument makers. The last entry was for zoos – with a myriad of opportunities to create animal and habitat smells to the brand's advantage. Given that just about every odour on the face of the earth can be manufactured in a laboratory today, there is almost always a way to use the sense of smell, no matter how small its application might be.

Remember, it is not the scale of how your aroma is used, and it is not the case that it has to be incorporated everywhere and in everything. Yes, the more you can utilise the smell, the more it can contribute to the brand experience. But even if you are limited to just one specific option – the reception area, or a piece of packaging – it really comes down to how creatively and consistently it is employed.

Let's take a company that makes healthcare equipment. It's likely that at least some part of the product is plastic. Today, almost any plastic part can have a scent incorporated into it. What kind of smell would the manufacturer want to use? If, for example, the units were sold directly to hospitals or surgeries, perhaps a clinical smell would be appropriate as an associative brand smell for both the healthcare operative and the patient.

On the other hand, if the product is sold directly to the public, the right smell might be the exact opposite of a clinical formula. For instance, I have a blood pressure monitor at home and prefer taking my own blood pressure readings rather than going to a doctor, where typically the 'white coat' effect often elevates the readouts. So, I wouldn't want the aroma of disinfectant or some other sterile smell to evoke what for me would be unpleasant memories of time spent in a waiting room or less than desirable blood pressure readings, but would find some other smell more satisfying – possibly the soothing effect of orange or lavender.

If you manufacture a product, one area that can definitely be enhanced is the packaging. Most products arrive in wrapping or binding that smells either of the material it's made from (in most cases cardboard or plastic) or, often, of stale cigarette smoke courtesy of the person who packed the goods. Either way, the packaging makes a statement about the overall brand not just through the visual sense (ie packaging design, colour scheme, shape, etc) but also by its smell. So, if the fragrance is malodorous, it's a smell-sense opportunity missed. With today's technology, every kind of packaging material from paper to polymers can have a particular aroma incorporated into its make-up. And if you can't utilise scented packaging, what about inks and varnishes used to print company details on it? Again, off-the-shelf smells are available, as are specially formulated signature scents.

Service with a smell

But what if I run a service, rather than make a product? For instance, I might be a sports instructor meeting clients at a stadium, pitch or sports facility that is not my own. What smells would I want to associate my brand with and how could they be used? Most likely, fragrances like cinnamon, lemon or jasmine would fit the bill as scents that evoke stimulating and energising feelings. But where would I use them? Well, I could consider spraying kit bags or other items that I might supply to my customers with an appropriate smell.

Or, instead of using a stimulating scent, I could incorporate the actual smell of the sports environment to form a strong association with the service I'm providing. Dale Air, mentioned earlier, has created a pack of 'football aroma' cubes featuring the smells of a football pitch, the trophy room – and even the players' changing room. For a football coach, or even soccer school, this could be a gift or sale item that would provide a creative way to enhance the company's brand.

And, of course, if it can be applied to football, it can be used with any other sport. The fragrance of willow, or the rich and nutty aroma of linseed oil, for cricket. Perhaps the leather smell of a catcher's glove in baseball. Or even the scent of a newly mown lawn at the Wimbledon tennis courts. We've already covered the advantages of spraying trainers with a particular smell. Truly, you are limited only by your imagination in how to make the sense of smell work for your brand.

Aromatic publicity and promotions

Did you ever see the movie *Legally Blonde*, in which Harvard law student Elle Woods (played by Reese Witherspoon) submits her résumé and says, 'It's pink, and scented. Don't you think it gives it that something extra?' Well, she was right. Adding a fragrance to your promotional items gives the recipient an extra sense to experience, offering another chance to put your brand into long-term memory. Don't, however, isolate the smell sense by using just one mailing or promotional item, or the connection to your brand will be weak. Far better to try to create a 'smell platform', where promotional activity using scent is built around a consistent theme.

Scented paper is one way to create a sense of smell in your mailings, or even a simple letterhead you may send out. But it needn't stop with just the paper. Products associated with perfumes, aftershaves and various personal toiletries have utilised scent samples in give-away bottles, vials and scent strips for many years – but there's no reason why such promotional opportunities should be limited to suppliers of eau de toilette. Since smells of any kind – from baby powder to cut grass, Cuban cigar smoke to sweaty feet – can now be concocted, the only real barrier is creativity. Let's consider two approaches to incorporating the sense of smell into your advertising and promotional materials:

1. **Direct product/service relevance.** By aligning the scent with the actual product or service, you give the customer a deeper sensory idea of using it. So, if you make pencils, sending out a mailer that includes a sachet or other container offering the smell of pencil or wood shavings enhances the whole promotional effect. If you run a travel agency, there are all kinds of fragrances available, including coconut, pineapple, tropical scents and even the smell of the sea to generate excitement and enthusiasm for the destinations you are promoting.

Plumbers can mail out fliers about blocked drains that include scented strips of a fresh smell like washing powder, carbolic soap or disinfectant. Or the approach could highlight what happens if blocked drains aren't cleared – using a small sachet that contains the smell of rotten fish or a stink bomb. Dental practitioners could use the smell of cloves or peppermint in a fresh breath campaign, and furniture renovators could utilise the fragrance of beeswax, oak or mahogany.

2. **Indirect novel link.** If you really and truly cannot find a way of using an aroma to describe direct aspects of your product or service, then try a novel way of involving scents and aromas. Use a play on words, an innuendo or a comic link to your offer. If you are making an offer that seems too good to be true, how about including the smell of bananas to suggest that's what you'd have to be to make such an offer?

If you want to highlight how your competitors seem to be offering a product or service under dubious terms, how about including a smell of fish to indicate 'something fishy going on'? All kinds of food-related and non-food-related smells can be used as metaphorical links to your campaigns. Perhaps I should have incorporated a sachet of ozone smell in this book to emphasise that when it comes to using scents in publicity and promotional materials, the sky's the limit.

Can you create a smell on your website? The answer is yes – well, using additional equipment, that is. You can send a signal to a unit connected to your PC that will then disperse a scent. One example of this is The Scent Dome from Trisenx (www.trinsenx.com). The Scent Dome is a computer peripheral device that releases different fragrances and aromas triggered by computer commands embedded in its accompanying software (as shown in Figure 10.1). These commands can be linked to e-mail, e-books, web pages and other digital content. Even a PowerPoint presentation can contain trigger codes to release scent at an appropriate slide. The unit, roughly the size of a teapot, generates smells by releasing particles from one or more of 20 liquid-filled odour capsules that can also mix with others to match the custom scent the user has created. Once triggered, The Scent Dome mixes the required cocktail of smells stored inside the fragrance canisters, and a small fan starts up and disperses the aroma through the air.

Figure 10.1 The Scent Dome: a computer peripheral for releasing aromas. Picture courtesy of TriSenx Holdings Inc. Used with permission

Containing the smell

If you don't want to take the 'live' scent approach, use the *novel link* alternative. In March 2007, Calvin Klein launched its CKIN2U unisex fragrance through the website Second Life (www.secondlife.com). This virtual-world website enabled visitors to pick up virtual bottles of the new scent and spray other in-world partners with fizzing fragrance bubbles to initiate dialogue. At the same time, UK consumers could click through to the CKIN2U website and request actual samples of the new fragrance.

Using sachets, glass or plastic tubes and other containers is a great way to provide the recipients with a sense of smell. The only downside is the unit cost per mailer, and the possibility that the storage device could get damaged in the mail. Happily, there is an alternative. With the advent of scratch-'n'-sniff technology in the late 1970s the door was opened for a multitude of opportunities to create true smell-sense experiences in promotional material that didn't need any container. Instead, the smell was impregnated into a coating that, when scratched, released the aroma. In the 1980s, scratch-'n'-sniff stickers were all the rage, and today some of those early examples fetch high prices on eBay. At that time, scratch-'n'-sniff advertisements were, like most sense-of-smell promotions, confined to perfume and aftershave products. Now that laboratories can create fragrances that mimic almost any kind of smell, the whole concept has opened up a multitude of possibilities.

Today, all kinds of publicity material can incorporate scratch-'n'-sniff devices, including press advertisements, promotional give-aways, postcards and inserts. For example, a number of gas supply companies have used a folded mailer containing a scratch-'n'-sniff strip impregnated with ethyl mercaptan, the 'rotten eggs' smell purposely added to odourless natural gas, to educate and inform customers about the dangers of gas leaks.

The drawback of scratch-'n'-sniff has always been that once the area is scratched, both the shelf life and the pass-along value of the item are limited. However, new technology has overcome that problem with the advent of scented varnishes. The clear varnish is applied over conventional litho printing inks, and the smell remains dormant until you rub it, after which it reverts to being dormant again until the next activation.

In 2007, specialist litho printing company Concord Litho, based in New Hampshire, created an interactive scent card insert for *TV Guide* magazine (see Figure 10.2). The insert was designed to treat fans of NBC's sitcom *My Name Is Earl* to a unique sensory experience: the quirky aromas of karma-obsessed Camden County. During the 'Laugh 'n' Sniff' episode, viewers were prompted to rub one of six corresponding numbered boxes on the scent card, which released aromas connected to the *My Name Is Earl* storyline, including the smell of a brand-new car, and the chocolatey-creamy signature scent of Oreo cookies.

Concord Litho has also created other items such as a promotional game piece for Domino's Pizza for its brownie bites product launch and a range of greetings cards featuring scents such as gingerbread, cookie, holiday pine and candy cane. Even if you are stuck for ideas of how to incorporate smells into your brand, the standard corporate card can be enhanced in this way.

Non-profit organisations can capitalise on this scent idea, too, as a compelling appeal to your donors. For instance, if you're a charity involved in providing aid to the Third World, you could depict the smells of poverty (see my sample in Figure 10.3) – perhaps even contrasting them with the fragrances of 'clean air' contained in another scent block. If your work is with nature conservation, can donors experience the smell of a tree, or the sound of wildlife? There are unlimited ways in which you can engage your donors in a deeper emotional experience.

Figure 10.2   Scented card examples from Concord Litho. Reproduced with permission

Your personal scent: good or bad idea?

One question I'm often asked is, 'Should you use a personal signature scent?' The example of Singapore Airlines would suggest that it could be very advantageous, depending on the circumstances. For most service companies, asking every employee in the office to wear a particular perfume or aftershave might well be met with a point-blank refusal – and it's certainly unnecessary if customers don't interface with them. (What's more, you could easily be flouting some human rights or image discrimination legislation!)

But if your staff are looking after an exhibition stand or serving customers in a showroom area, a consistent personal scent could certainly raise awareness. What would be confusing, however, is to create a showroom or exhibition

Every day in Dharavi, this child wakes up
to the smell of poverty.

Rub here to experience it for yourself.
If you can stomach it.

hElp+mumbAi
POVERTY RELIEF

Figure 10.3 An example of how a scented card could be used for a non-profit donor mailing

stand aroma and then limit its usability by swamping it with conflicting smells so that the customer leaves feeling confused about the sense of smell experience.

One situation where a consistent personal aftershave or perfume could be a significant part of your brand perception is if you are a one-person operation, or you are the only one who deals with customers on a face-to-face basis. Martin Lindstrom states that his very reason for conducting research on sensory branding came from an encounter in the street with a passer-by:

> We must return to the basics and identify what actually appeals to human beings on an ordinary, everyday basis. The answer on a practical level, though, came to me on a Tokyo street in the spring of 1999. A lady brushed by me and her perfume took me back to my childhood. It was extraordinary. For a moment the rush-hour crowds, the traffic and the high-rise buildings ceased to exist. I was instantly transported to the Danish countryside,

smelling the same perfume that a friend of mine always wore. It stood to reason that if brands contained a scent, they could be equally powerful.

If image is important in a company sense, it is absolutely critical if you are a lone entrepreneur, where using every image tool at your disposal can help create a sensory cue for your brand – your personal brand. As Lindstrom recounts, just an awareness of a scent can evoke emotions, and using an appropriate perfume or aftershave can give you a business edge. Studies have shown that perfumes and colognes can give strong impressions of financial success and high levels of self-confidence. Such is the power of the sense of smell that even if the fragrance is fleeting, the memories evoked and resultant emotions remain.

Using an aftershave or perfume as part of your brand will demand careful selection of the appropriate smell according to the image you want associated with it. Light, flowery fragrances will convey a different impression from the spicier types, just as much as when they are used in other business situations. But there are additional considerations, such as how the smell actually works on your particular skin and whether the fragrance might be too strong when you wear it. Using aftershaves, colognes and perfumes in this way needs subtlety. There is nothing worse than trying to engage in a business dialogue when someone is so drenched in a smell that it smothers everyone and everything in the room. Also, the use of personal scents needs to be considered in the wider context of your overall image, grooming and wardrobe.

For individual advice in personal branding, check out your local image or personal branding consultant.

Use scents and aromas with care

Just as music levels in a retail or reception environment can be overpowering and a customer turn-off rather than enhancement, fragrances need to be used with care, too. Companies using scents in their marketing have sometimes been accused of damaging the nation's health by ignoring those with allergies to certain smells.

A couple of years ago the California Milk Processor Board launched an outdoor poster campaign in San Francisco for milk, featuring scented strips that gave off a fresh cookie smell. Within a short time the campaign was dropped after city officials claimed that the aroma could trigger allergies and asthma attacks. Evidence that this is the case has yet to be confirmed. While some studies assert that up to 72 per cent of asthmatic attacks are triggered by a fragrance, panels of scent experts have disputed these claims, contending that there are no hard facts to support these allegations. Instead, they argue, people are reacting psychologically to the ingredients that would normally be there in the 'real' product but are not actually present in the scent.

The key, of course, is to ensure that your customers are put 'in control' of being able to leave a scented area, or able to push or not push the scent spray button at the point of sale. This was the main problem with the San Francisco milk campaign: the person waiting for the bus did not have the option to move away. Taking away customer choice, as in this case, is exactly the opposite of what we want to do with our sensory brand approach.

Regardless of who's right in the allergy debate, you do need to ensure that customers are not overwhelmed with scents. Even those who don't suffer from allergic reactions can still find it obnoxious to walk around in a fragrance-drenched area, whether it's a retail outlet, showroom or reception area. A small amount diffused into the air will have a much greater effect than soaking customers in it.

Without a doubt, the sense of smell is there to be exploited as part of your brand experience. And with so many aromas now available, your customers won't just wake up and smell the coffee; they can wake up to just about any smell you decide.

11

Branding the taste buds

It's probably not surprising that when it comes to discussing the sense of taste, books and articles generally combine it with the sense of smell. Taste really does need the nose to be involved if the full spectrum of tastes and flavours are to be experienced. When food or drink enters the mouth, taste and smell are sent as integrated signals to the brain in order to process taste sensations. Although the tongue has receptors that can detect tastes, without smell it is limited to just five. (That's why if you're suffering from a cold, or you simply pinch your nose while eating or drinking, your taste discernment fades rapidly.) The first four stand-alone tastes are the traditional sensations of sweet, sour, salty and bitter. However, in 1908 a Japanese scientist discovered that a type of glutamic acid called monosodium glutamate was responsible for a particular savoury taste that is now classified as the fifth taste sense, called umami.

Getting the edge in food and drink

In terms of sensory experience, taste is often considered to be the most difficult to incorporate into a business brand. Of course, if your trade is to do with food and drink, there are many opportunities to create emotions and push your brand into long-term memory simply by what you have on offer. So, as the saying goes, if you've got it, flaunt it. Make sure that the taste element of your food is utilised wherever and whenever you can. If you operate a food or drink outlet, hand out samples of new menu or recipe items to passers-by. Themed evenings where guests can try the food or drink are a great way to build your brand, as they give you an ideal opportunity to utilise the other four senses in creating the customer experience.

Gordon Ramsay OBE is a chef who has demonstrated how to build a powerful brand in both the United Kingdom and the United States not just by demonstrating his supreme skills as a master chef but also by using these talents as a launch pad for other activities. Gordon has written books on various food topics and starred in a number of television series where he not only prepares sumptuous food but also acts as troubleshooter for ailing restaurants and helps them to recover their trading position. Ramsay's company now boasts restaurants, media and consultancy businesses on both sides of the Atlantic.

If you run a single restaurant and you want to improve your brand, can you compete with Gordon? Probably not, but you don't have to. What's important is that you look at the kinds of things he's done and consider how your business might do the same thing, albeit on a smaller scale. For example:

- You may not command a series on a national television network, but you could gain a regular spot on your local radio station talking about food and drink, providing phone-in recipes.
- You could offer your local newspaper or magazine articles built around helpful tips on how to select a good wine, or what dishes comprise the best three-course meal.
- You could create co-promotions with the station or newspaper so that people could come to food and wine sampling sessions, or even offer a free meal at your restaurant for a competition winner.

A tasty non-food business

This is all well and good for those in the food and drink market. But what happens if you make nuts and bolts in a factory unit on some industrial estate and apart from your brochures and price lists have only some display cabinets in your reception area with which to communicate with clients and potential new buyers?

Let's remind ourselves that generating a full sensory customer experience does not mean that every sense can be used at every customer interface – nor is it necessary. Neither does it follow that the sense must be a direct aspect of your product or service. It is not about how many, or how often, but more about consistency and creativity when it is incorporated.

Let me give you an example. I once worked for a large United Kingdom-based corporation and was responsible for reviewing its supplier list of graphic design consultancies. There were over 40 companies that supplied this blue-chip giant, but the brief was to cut it down to just 7. For a number of weeks I visited each design outfit in turn. The meetings became predictable quite quickly. First there would be a lengthy and boring presentation about the design company and its staff credentials, followed by an endless display of successful projects carried out for others. Then, finally, there followed a short question-and-answer session about what they could do for us if they were retained. The structure of these meetings was bad enough – self-indulgent and not much thought for the customer. I was only able to stay awake because someone would usually arrive with cups of tea or coffee, and a few chocolate chip cookies melting in the saucer, which provided a short break from the proceedings.

Then one morning I arrived at a small design studio in London. Before I even climbed the stairs, the smell of freshly ground coffee hit me. A polite receptionist greeted me and handed me a card that featured several options for refreshments. It read like a wine bar menu! Coffee, tea, soft drinks... each with a short, mouth-watering description of what was on offer. I gave my 'order' to the receptionist.

When I walked into the meeting room a few minutes later, my drink was already waiting for me and next to it a small fortune cookie with my name on the wrapper. The message inside the cookie said, 'James, today is a great day for a positive business meeting.' I ate the cookie and it tasted delicious. What followed was indeed a good meeting, where they spent much more time talking about my company's wants and needs rather than focusing on their own achievements.

Now, this design company was small compared to most of the others on the supplier list. They weren't restaurant owners, nor did they make fortune cookies. But that single encounter with their approach to refreshments communicated volumes about their whole attitude to customers and for me a true understanding of how every sensory perception can be used to differentiate the brand. Of course, their 'product' had to be good, but I wouldn't even have been there if it wasn't. When the time came to make a decision as to who stayed on the list as a supplier and who didn't, how do you think they fared?

Sweet ways to brand your business

Using tastes and flavours in your business can be something as simple as the example above. Why not have a bowl of sweets or mints (with personalised wrappers) in your reception and showroom areas – or on your exhibition stand? If you don't greet customers on your premises, then send them some hand-made chocolates or other items of confectionery that include your company name and have some connection with your brand. It's even possible to obtain edible chocolate business cards that could be sent out to prospective new customers along with the usual printed card version.

For most businesses the best way of promoting the brand, product or service using taste is the novel link, as it is with smell. Whether your marketing activity features jelly beans or toffee jars, the point is to try to associate the taste with an aspect of your brand, product or service. Like the themed evening example mentioned earlier, you could hold regular customer evenings as a way of thanking your customers for their patronage, and inviting prospective clients along too. Most businesses that do this serve food and drink that may taste good but that fail to make a connection with the brand. Yet just a personalised label on the wine bottles can be enough to form a brand link. One step further is to accompany each bottle with a swing ticket, perhaps associating the wine description with your product or service's brand characteristics. Here are some other options:

- A construction company or security firm might serve a full-bodied red wine and associate this with an aspect of the company's strength.
- An art gallery might create a special cocktail and name it after the business (check out www.baileys.com for some very interesting ways to use Baileys Irish Cream in cocktails, for example).
- Non-alcoholic drinks can also be linked to your brand through descriptions and metaphors relating to taste. For instance, if you're launching a new product or service, how about sending out some cola, cordial or sparkling mineral water with a personalised label and an accompanying message that says something like, 'If you think this is refreshing, you should try our new…' There are countless other connections.

Remember, the objective here is to link a taste to an aspect of your brand. This is not the same as sending out some bottles of wine or boxes of chocolates merely as one-off gifts that are unrelated to your brand activities. This is a part of the sensory experience you wish to create, and as long as it can be packaged and posted without leaking, or damaging any other contents of the mailing, you can send almost anything. (Ensure that any food and drink items are properly and legally labelled. If you're mailing nuts, for example, be aware that some people have nut allergies. You want to delight your customers, not make them ill.)

Here are some food and drink items I've used successfully in direct mail campaigns that you can incorporate as a taste-sense connection in your business. I'll leave you to work out possible associations.

personalised sauce sachets (hot, mild, cool)
lemons
sparkling water
mints
crisps
nuts
isotonic energy drinks
packets of raisins
tea bags
Easter eggs
lollipops (personalised with a message)
popcorn
bananas
cheese
toffee
chewing gum/bubble gum
crackers
marshmallows
miniature champagnes or
  spirits
packet soup
chocolate bars
jelly beans
rock (personalised with
  name running down
  centre)
apples

You needn't limit your materials for your sense of taste promotions to drinks. TMB (The Marketing Bureau) in the United Kingdom wanted to promote the hire of executive boxes at AFC Bournemouth's football stadium. The football club is known as the Cherries, so TMB sent a direct-mail package that included cherries to key business decision makers.

The package led the recipients to a micro-site specially created to provide further information and handle resultant enquiries. The mailing achieved a staggering 70 per cent response rate.

Taste buds and business tie-ins

Customers do not necessarily have to sample food or drink to connect it with a product. Using the *novel link* approach, just a strong creative association – if done well – can be enough to engage the sense of taste and make a connection. An excellent example of this is the television advertising campaign created in 2007 by London advertising agency Fallon for the launch of Škoda's new – at the time – Fabia.

The agency wanted to get across the point that the car was 'tasty', so they baked a life-sized cake car that looked just like the real thing. Rivets were swapped for raisins and spark plugs for sugar. Some of the United Kingdom's finest chocolatiers, bakers and bricklayers were enlisted to construct the cake car, which was made using hundreds of kilos of raw material. The radiators were constructed from chocolate blocks, headlights were made from boiled sweets, fog lights from meringue and door mirrors from marzipan. Figures 11.1–11.6 show some clips from the television commercial, which ends with the strapline 'The new Fabia. Full of lovely stuff.'

The promotion didn't just end with television advertising. A through-the-line campaign was also developed, including point-of-sale and dealership materials continuing the theme of the Fabia being so 'moreish' and how much extra you got from the tasty new model. The promotions included sending out air fresheners with a chocolate aroma to tie in with the cake concept.

The publicity resulting from the campaign was exceptional, with coverage in all the national media – in some cases double-page spreads featuring numerous stage-by-stage stills of the car being constructed.

As if that wasn't a success in itself, extra media coverage was given to what happened to the food once filming was finished. Fallon and Škoda had planned to cut the cake car up and distribute it to local charities, schools and hospitals. Unfortunately, as the car had been under hot studio lights for several days, it would have posed a health risk if eaten. Some parts, such as the marzipan wing mirrors and chocolate speedometer were preserved, while the rest of the car was composted and used by residents of Clapton, east London, to fertilise their gardens and allotments.

According to Škoda, the number of visitors to its car dealerships was up by 160 per cent in the first week of the campaign compared to the previous year. It's obvious to all that the cake car campaign made a significant contribution to such impressive statistics.

OK, you're a smaller business than Škoda and you don't have the money to put a television commercial together, let alone one that involves more

Figure 11.1 Chocolate mix – clip from the Škoda Fabia TV campaign. All stills courtesy of Fallon London Ltd and Škoda. Reproduced with permission

Figure 11.2 Engine oil

Figure 11.3 Rear light

Figure 11.4 Tyres

Figure 11.5   End frame of TV ad

Figure 11.6   Along with the Skoda TV campaign, this humorous direct mail pack tapped into the confectionery theme by featuring a car-shaped chocolate fudge-scented air freshener. Picture courtesy archibald ingall stretton. Used with permission

ingredients than you consume in an entire year. The point is, you can still create successful sensory perceptions of taste on much smaller budgets. Chocolates, miniature drinks and packets of personalised mints are not that expensive. They don't have to be original recipes, either, if you cannot afford to go down that route. What's most important is how you use these items.

The key, as with most things in branding, is connection and association. Get it right, and your brand experience will leave a nice taste in your customers' mouths.

12

Brand touch and feel

We've all been to stores where the 'do not touch' notices outnumber the goods on display twice over. What a turn-off. Granted, some objects are fragile and expensive to replace, so 'hands off' notices may be unavoidable. But this should definitely be the exception rather than the rule. Not being able to touch something is contrary to the way human beings are wired. For out of all the senses we possess, touch is the most basic. It's the first sense we experience when still in the womb and it's the last one we lose before death.

Very often, touching a product is second only to the visual sense as a precursor to purchasing it. We squeeze a fruit to 'feel' its freshness. We put a towel to our face to experience its softness. We press our hands down on a mattress to test its springiness. And although functionality is part of the purchase consideration, our tactile examination of the goods will be a key factor – one linked to our personality and our social and lifestyle wants and needs.

For instance, writing a note to someone can be done with a cheap, throwaway ballpoint pen. You don't care what it feels like, or even how it looks, as long as it does the job. But when it comes to choosing a writing instrument that reflects style and personality, a fine pen such as a Mont Blanc is in a totally different league. You'll want to experience how it feels between the fingers of your writing hand. You'll explore the texture of the barrel and cap, feeling the weight of the pen's body as you make those initial sweeps of the words you write. And as you do, these physical pleasures evoke strong emotions and feelings. It's the same with a watch. If telling the time were the only function required of a wristwatch, companies such as Rolex or Cartier would be low on sales! But when you stroke your fingers over the gold case, or feel the platinum bezel surrounding the watch face, emotions begin to rise that have nothing to do with times and dates.

As with many of the other senses, however, small businesses have been slow to pick up on the advantages of including this fifth sense in their branding. With the advent of the fast-route-to-purchase online store, a lot of companies have assumed that the sense of touch is far less important today. After all, you can't incorporate touch into a website, can you? (Actually, it is possible in a way. We'll cover that later.) But there are still many customers out there who visit shops where products can be touched and examined before a purchase is made. They'll want to try on their next pair of hand-made shoes, walk a few paces to feel how comfortable they are, and brush their fingers across the detailed stitching and polished leather before placing their order.

Getting in touch with your brand

Our sense of touch, then, is anything but redundant. The skin's millions of sensory receptors are there ready and waiting to explore shape, weight and texture. In addition, we can sense heat, vibration and pressure. And it's not just our hands that are sensitive to these elements of touch. All parts of the body contain sensory receptors. Consider how we experience the feel of a deep pile carpet beneath our feet, the comfort of a leather recliner or the softness of fur as it brushes against our face. Even without the benefit of other senses such as sight, there is much we can discover simply by using our touch sense alone. Those who are visually impaired rely heavily on their ability to detect the world around them using touch, which is often attuned to respond more sensitively than for people with the added advantage of sight.

If you run a business that manufactures or sells products, here's an exercise. Reach inside your food cupboard at home, either without looking or with your eyes closed, and see how easily you can identify the products and their respective brands purely by touch. When I've tried this, I usually end up recognising just two items: a bottle of olive oil (taller than all the other bottles, so I know what it is and who makes it) and a jar of Marmite (see the photograph of my cupboard in Figure 12.1). The shape of the Marmite jar has remained pretty much the same since it was introduced in 1920, and it is immediately identifiable in any touch-only test. (For North American readers, Marmite is a savoury spread that's a real breakfast and sandwich favourite in the United Kingdom.)

So now let's ask: if you run a business that manufactures or sells products, could your customers differentiate your products from those of your competitors – with their eyes closed and relying on touch alone? Of course,

Figure 12.1   Bottles and jars from my food cupboard. The marmite jar stands out from them all

if you supply huge industrial gas turbines, then this simple test may need modifying! But even with large engineering products there is always the opportunity for some part of the design or structure to contain an engraved metal plate, raised plastic lettering or your logo etched into a particular surface area of your product that gives a sense-of-touch clue as to what brand is behind it. All too often, such identification is merely a small stamped plate riveted on to the back of the unit, complete with serial or part number, tucked away for no one to find until there's a problem. What a way to treat a brand.

So how do we determine the best way to use the sense of touch for our products? There are two basic routes to take:

> 1. Use product design features to differentiate your brand from the competition.

Product design has changed dramatically over the past 30 years or so. Prior to this, functionality was often the only area of focus for a product designer. Even then, the design was conceived more as a concept in the mind of the designer than through discovering what the end user really wanted.

Add an emotional touch to your product

The customer's heightened expectations today mean that functionality is a given. And, as we've discovered throughout this book, emotional benefits are more important than ever before. Product design is now approached using sophisticated methodologies, including kansei engineering, meaning that the functional aspects of a product are balanced against the desire for emotional expressiveness.

Although the vast subject of product design is way beyond the scope of this book, we can ask some simple questions that might evoke a deeper consideration of how well thought out your product's tactile features are. For example, what does your product convey in terms of its shape? Does it have traditional contours or is it contemporary in form – and how do either of these relate to your brand? A modern-shaped product backed by a traditional brand identity could create confusion, just as a traditional product shape that conveys years of experience will if it's made by a business whose brand is modern and flashy.

What about the surface on your product? Is it plain or textured, coated or uncoated? Does it make me want to run my fingers over the front, back and sides? What do I feel when I touch the dials, buttons or switches? What does each press, push or slide action convey about your brand? Even if you manufacture what some might consider a mundane industrial product, there must be some way in which you can enhance the tactile experience, no matter how small in comparison to the total unit. For example:

- If your type of product usually has a matt surface, what would happen if you used a gloss surface, even for just a part of it?
- If all the dials and switches are of standard touch and feel, could you include one – a special one – that felt different in terms of tactile response? If so, you could use this as a brand identifier, because none of your competitors would have such an addition.

Think about how Apple has really scored major points in touch and feel with its iPod series. Place any number of MP3 players on a table alongside an iPod and, using the closed-eyes test again, see how easy it is to distinguish the Apple brand simply by feeling its contours, its surface and the quality of its four click-wheel buttons, the tactile feedback of which is like no other. Even without an Apple logo in sight, it has Apple written all over it.

Some time ago, I spilled a cup of coffee on to my PC keyboard and it stopped functioning. As an emergency solution I had to purchase a very low-priced, unbranded keyboard from the local store (it was all they had in stock) until I could order a proper replacement. No wonder the keyboard didn't feel worthy of a brand identifier. The keys were totally unresponsive. The spacebar had no spring to it. Its design felt uncomfortable when I placed my hands in position to type. Even the transfers on the keys that showed the various letters of the alphabet felt like sandpaper.

I breathed a sigh of relief when I took delivery of my top-brand keyboard. With its stylish contours it felt modern and very comfortable to use. Its keys were a joy to press. I felt them respond to even the gentlest of pressure, while their engraved tops gave me an extra tactile experience under my fingertips as I typed. The attachable wrist rest provided additional comfort and the whole keyboard just assured me that here was a brand that really thought about its end user.

As I ran my fingers over the logo proudly embossed in a vivid blue rubber square that stood out from the surrounding surfaces, I knew that I could stay with this brand for a very long time.

A product's shape, texture and weight can dramatically affect the perception of the company that produces it. If, for health and safety reasons, or certain rules governing product design in your particular industry, you are forced to keep to a specific design that looks like everyone else's, then at least consider how you might include your logo in a creative tactile way. In a market of increasingly look-alike products, that alone may be enough for you to stand out from the crowd.

> 2. Create a connection between the product's tactile packaging and the brand itself. In other words, the packaging becomes a basic brand identifier.

In the fiercely competitive retail world, getting your product to stand out on the shelves is a constant challenge. Yet just the look and feel of a product's packaging can become a key brand differentiator and sales booster. Studies have shown that even if a tactile experience from the packaging has no direct bearing on any feature or benefit relating to the product inside, sales may still increase. The perfume industry recognised a long time ago that although consumers buy products, they experience the packaging first. After all, who would think of purchasing an expensive aftershave or perfume if the packaging didn't denote its status? Would you buy an opulent jewellery item as a gift if the box it came in was anything less than velvet-lined?

For many years, companies in the luxury goods market gained enormous brand differentiation advantages with their packaging, while most other businesses focused on the logistics and functional side (for example, how secure was the item, how many could be stacked on a pallet and so on). Anything else was simply – if you'll pardon the pun – cosmetic. And expensive, too. But now, with the enormous strides in printing and packaging technology that have taken place, any business can give product packaging a tactile experience that provides brand identification – and it needn't cost the earth.

Consider, first, the contour and shape of your packaging and how this alone can become a major brand identifier. Take bottles, for example. In 1916 the Root Glass Company based in Indiana designed what was to turn into the world-famous Coca-Cola glass bottle (shown in Figure 12.2). The brief from Coca-Cola was twofold: first, the bottle needed to be recognisable as a Coca-Cola bottle even in complete darkness; and second, if the bottle were broken, a person still had to be able to tell what it was – and what brand owned it. Even though throughout the years competitors such as Virgin Cola have produced their own similar versions (Virgin launched its cola drink in 1996 and used a bottle design allegedly inspired by the shape of *Baywatch* star Pamela Anderson), nothing has really replaced the timeless design of the original Coke bottle.

In August 2007, Coca-Cola in the United Kingdom commissioned Sir Peter Blake, one of the leading lights of the pop art movement in the 1960s,

Figure 12.2   The world-famous original Coca-Cola 'Classic' bottle. Photograph reproduced with permission

to create a huge piece of art on London's South Bank featuring the famous bottle, coinciding with the company's sponsorship of the British Film Institute's Andy Warhol film season. Warhol was another famous 1960s artist who painted several works of art highlighting the iconic Coca-Cola bottle. (I mention this event because it shows precisely how you can gain immense leverage when you have a winning combination of sensory connections. Just think of all the public relations opportunities and media coverage Coca-Cola has managed to obtain for getting close to 100 years since the introduction of that classic bottle.)

Glass is only one of many materials that can be given a unique shape. In 1993, Coca-Cola introduced a version of its contoured bottle made from polyethylene terephthalate (PET), a thermoplastic polyester that's much lighter than glass, and environmentally friendly. In 2000 the company began using the even lighter Ultra-Glass contour bottle, which gave improved impact resistance and reduced production costs.

In 2007, Evian® Natural Spring Water, part of the Danone Group, launched its luxury Palace Bottle™ in North America. Aimed specifically at the fine dining market, where bottled water brands compete largely on the basis of innovative packaging, the bottle was designed to represent the modern Evian brand but at the same time maintain a strong tie to its source in the French Alps.

The Palace Bottle shape is sleek and contemporary, and has an etched 'mountain-top' relief design towards its base (see Figure 12.3). Along with the bottle, Evian produced a unique pouring instrument called the Palace Pourer. The pourer not only prevents splashing as the water is poured but also provides customers with a special experience of ordering and decanting a bottle of water in style. As Caroline Kibler, brand manager of Evian North America, says, 'I see packaging taking on a larger and larger role as consumers continue to have more options and feel empowered to demand packaging forms that fit their every usage occasion.' Clearly, the Palace Bottle would have no problem in passing the 'touch-only' test to determine the brand behind it.

Figure 12.3 Evian's Palace Bottle™. Photograph courtesy of Evian® Natural Spring Water

Of course, shape applies to all kinds of packaging formats, not just bottles. Thanks to modern die-cutting and creasing technology, cardboard or plastic cartons do not have to be limited to square or oblong shapes. Sharp curves, zigzags, concertina-like folds and cut-outs can all change the shape of packaging from drab to fab.

Consider the famous Toblerone triangular box. If Coca-Cola's contoured bottle is the benchmark packaging for a soft drink, then Toblerone's cardboard carton is the equivalent in confectionery packaging. What's interesting is that both have been easy to adapt to shifting trends over the years without making any significant changes to their overall shape. Whether your packaging is made from card, glass, metal or fabric, there are plenty of opportunities to create a tactile experience that helps define your brand. Perhaps it's time to take a look at your product packaging and see what shape it's in.

Bringing your brand to the surface

Along with shape, texture also provides a way to reach out to the consumer via the touch sense. Research conducted by the School of Mechanical Engineering at the University of Leeds showed evidence of a link between the texture of a cosmetic bottle and a positive consumer reaction, namely that a smoother surface increased the perception of stylishness when measured against a rougher surface. This not only shows that tactile qualities can alter a perception about the product but also introduces the prospect of aligning a surface texture with a brand personality.

Here are a few ideas that can encourage customers to respond to the touch and feel of packaging:

- Most packaging materials can incorporate surface simulations that include metal, suede, silk, wood and fabric surfaces. Find the surface that provides the right sense of touch to relate to your particular brand. Some years ago, when Universal Studios marketed its *Scarface* 'Limited' Deluxe Edition DVD in the United States, it used printing and embossing techniques to cover the entire case in black imitation snakeskin (the 'scales' of the reptile could be felt as your hand stroked the box). The whole tactile experience evoked feelings of masculinity and danger, perfectly reflecting the theme of the movie. If your brand operates in a 'masculine' market, what surface or texture could you utilise to convey your brand personality? Or, if you serve a predominantly female market, what soft-surface options would provide the best sensory cue?

- Where appropriate, use polypropylene packaging. It's a versatile and recyclable material that allows the creation of excellent tactile packaging ideas. It can be transparent, with etched or embossed inks highlighting the brand or product details, or frosted, with just your logo picked out in the clear material. Again, the touch experience can be associated with the personality of your brand: strong, professional, trustworthy, etc.

- Blister and clamshell packing not only offers excellent product visibility but its form and shape alone can separate your brand from the rest (it's the 'closed eyes' test again). The blister pack can also take advantage of ink and varnish technology to enhance its surface feel. The blister itself will obviously be moulded to hold the product. That doesn't mean you can't reserve a particular part of it just for the logo, which can be embossed or engraved into the plastic.

- If your packaging is of necessity very plain (eg off-the-shelf bubble wrap or standard corrugated cardboard boxes), consider using a tactile address label to add a sense of touch. Embossing, gold foil blocking or varnishing can still provide a point of difference. Or if you are into conservation and environmental concerns, the use of a recycled and basic carton may be just the thing to unite its tactile quality with your brand.

- Braille became mandatory on packaging for pharmaceutical use in European countries from September 2006. But why not incorporate it as an additional extra in your own packaging? Apart from assisting those with visual impairment, the embossed Braille icons create a unique tactile pattern, as well as showing that you are a socially responsible business that cares about accessibility and inclusion.

- In all of these areas, consider how you could leverage the tactile experience for use in other parts of your business. If you use a highly varnished packaging approach, how could that same gloss feel be applied in, say, your promotional materials, or your showroom area? We've covered the importance of consistency in the use of the senses, and touch is no exception.

Branding on the can

Although PET bottles are widely used as drinks containers, the steel and aluminium can is still a favourite packaging device. With modern technology offering many different printing options, it's possible to create an array of tactile finishes that spruce up any 'flat' can of the kind that's often used.

For example, to mark the Rugby World Cup in 2003, Ball Packaging Europe created a tactile beer can for Heineken that used embossing techniques to depict the traditional rugby shirts worn by players (see Figure 12.4). Even the shirt buttons featured on the cans were true to the original. Another example of an embossed can from Ball Packaging Europe is for Polish beer brand Żywiec (Figure 12.5). The can's embossing emphasises the brewery's coat of arms and gives the can a superior feel, highlighting the quality of both the beer and the brand.

■ Finishes other than embossing can also be used to add a highly tactile experience. A special combination of ink and varnish can create a 'soft touch' feel to metal containers, while other combinations can give an orange-peel surface effect. Letters and numbers can be engraved on both ends, and the tabs for opening can be incised with a picture, symbol or character. So, just on a simple container like a can, there is much that can be added to give the sense of touch a real boost.

As with the other four senses, creativity is a major key here. It's not just what materials, inks and varnishes you use, it's how you use them. Sometimes making the entire packaging surfaces a tactile experience will be just what is needed. In other situations, less is more, and a small, subtle application of varnish, embossing or other enhancement will be all that's required. Only you can determine which route to go, depending on the type of business you run and the product you are packaging. The important thing is that you include at least something tactile to give to your customers.

Using touch in a service business

Let's now consider companies or non-profits that provide a service rather than a product (although in fact these ideas are applicable to both). If you fit into this category, how can you exploit the sense of touch? The most obvious area is that of promotional materials. Here are some hints and tips on including a tactile cue in your collateral:

Figure 12.4 Embossed Heineken beer cans for the Rugby World Cup 2003. Courtesy of Ball Packaging Europe. Used with permission

Figure 12.5 Żywiec beer also uses embossing to highlight its brand. Courtesy of Ball Packaging Europe. Used with permission

- Consider brochures, for example. The application of spot varnish to accentuate specific parts of a brochure's contents is pretty much old hat nowadays, but it's still extremely effective as a sense of touch mechanism. There are a myriad of other ink or varnish combinations, too. In addition, consider die stamping, engraving or thermography, which creates raised printing. There are so many options for crafting something special in printed materials today.

None of these print variations need be expensive. For very short runs, you could even incorporate some do-it-yourself enhancements. As a favour to a friend who ran a very up-market but small financial services consultancy, I produced a mailer that was closed with gold sealing wax impressed with an off-the-shelf stamp of the first letter in the firm's name. The use of the wax was combined with a quality parchment-like paper texture, and the feel of the whole mailer conveyed quality and experience, evoking emotions of confidence and trust.

Even though the mailing was 'cold' in that it went out to a completely unqualified list of potential customers, it generated a response of over 70 per cent. Many of the new clients remarked how the feel of the mailing piece was so different from those normally received, so much so that they kept returning to it throughout the day it was received to 're-experience' its overall feel.

Because the mailing was limited to around a hundred rich-list prospects, the company did the sealing wax part itself in a two-hour session with just a couple of staff. The cost of the wax sticks and a few brass seals was minuscule compared to the income generated by mailing.

- But remember: one swallow doesn't make a summer. It was essential that the firm carried this tactile approach through to other aspects of its brand presentation. The owner of the business held a welcome evening for the new clients, where he gave them all a complimentary bottle of wine in an off-the-shelf decorative carrier bag sealed with... you guessed it, sealing wax. A small swing-card attached to the wine bottle thanking them for becoming a new customer was created using the same parchment texture as in the mailing.

   The reception area featured various blow-up pictures of the mailer and seal, accompanied by captions using puns such as 'Stick with us...' and 'Business that's signed, delivered and sealed...'. OK, it was rather cheesy. But the point is, the whole branding exercise worked because the success of the fifth sensory cue was purposely connected to the other four senses to create a total customer experience. This whole experiential theme relating to the brand continued for five years, when the firm was acquired for a substantial sum by a major financial services company.

■ Promotional materials can also include tactile samples to convey the sense of touch relating to the service being offered. Whether it be novelties that connect to the brand through metaphors and allusions or actual items relating to the service, a sense of touch means the recipient can experience the tactile dimension on a personal level. References via a play on words can be made to all kinds of objects that convey a brand or product/service quality, or knock the competition for their weakness in a particular area.

Consider tactile words like *dull, straight, edge, curve, spongy, springy, bumpy, soft, slimy, silky, velvety, rough, coarse, rigid* and *flexible*. Is your company 'flexible' in accommodating customer specifications? Then don't just say it, link it to a flexible object that you include in the mailing. I'm sure you get the point.

Charities can benefit from a tactile approach

Not-for-profit organisations can use items to convey issues relating to the cause they support. For example, in 2006 the United Kingdom-based firm Whitewater, a leading direct marketing agency specialising in non-profit causes, created a mailpack for Practical Action, a charity involved in poverty reduction in the developing world (see Figure 12.6). Aimed at high-value donors, the pack contained the usual letter and background material and donation form.

But in addition, the mailing included a 6-inch length of 8mm galvanised steel cable. As Nick Couldry, creative director of Whitewater, pointed out, 'The steel cable added an extra dimension to the mailer. Donors could hold in their hands what their money was helping to buy.' The pack resulted in a donor response that beat the target income by 59 per cent. The pack was also a finalist in the 2006 Direct Marketing Association ECHO Awards.

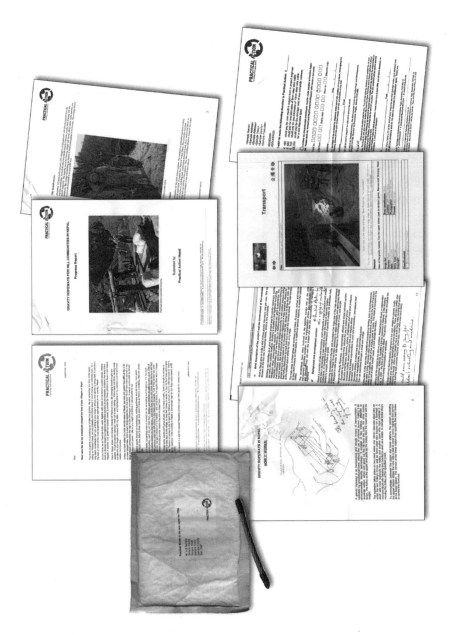

Figure 12.6 Charities, too, can benefit from a tactile approach: a mailpack for Practical Action

It's your turn to be tactile

Put your creative hat on and try this mental exercise. Consider how you could communicate your brand values in a mailer that included one of the following items:

square of fabric (leather, velvet, fur, etc)
button
piece of balsa wood
candle
flower
sponge
pair of chopsticks
shoelace
magic wand
hot water bottle

Let's take the chopsticks as a possible mailpack item (duly personalised with your company logo and details, of course). Given that many people (including clients and potential clients) who like eating Chinese food still can't use chopsticks properly, you could mail out a pair of chopsticks along with a small leaflet showing how to get to grips with them. This 'educational good turn' could have a strong link to a particular part of your company's service, whether it be an emphasis on your brilliant customer support, your super training department or the quality of your technical manuals.

Can you imagine the recipients in their offices at lunchtime, playing around with those chopsticks, reading the instructions, perhaps even showing off to someone else how they've suddenly perfected the art – and all of this revolving around your brand?

But you mustn't stop there, because you want to create enough leverage to push the brand into long-term memory, not just create a one-off promotion (which is often what happens with small business campaigns). What if you held a competition for the recipient who could pick up a grain of rice the fastest, and offered a high-quality wok as a prize (as in Figure 12.7)? What if you tied this promotion to a local charity that could benefit in some way from the proceeds? For example, hire some Chinese cooks (you could do this at low cost through a joint promotion) to prepare food and invite local homeless people to a meal on the house. Of course, you'd make sure the press were there to provide media coverage. It's a win–win–win situation for the

Figure 12.7 Possible campaign involving the sense of touch

customers, the charity and your brand. All from a small tactile item that you can buy for next to nothing.

Think about all the other promotional opportunities where form, shape and feel can be applied. For instance, display stands, brochure holders, leaflet dispensers, posters, signage, presentation folders and corporate stationery are strong contenders for a tactile dimension. All can take advantage of the various print, embossing and engraving techniques we've just discussed, to give additional follow-through from your other promotional materials.

Tactile books are used widely in education because they stimulate and engage young children in exploring the meaning of words through textures and shapes. Why not consider producing a tactile book to promote your business and enhance your brand? Paper engineering and book printing today allow your customers the opportunity to carry out tactile activities such as pulling, lifting, stroking and even shaking. What if your instruction manuals, for instance, were tactile, rather than flat and one-dimensional?

Touching what surrounds you

Whether you sell products or services, you need to consider the touch sense in your customer environments. Give some thought to your reception or showroom area in terms of surfaces and shapes. For example:

- What kind of tactile designs best reflect the brand you want to portray? Solid lines or jagged lines, curves or rounded corners?
- What about furniture? There's nothing worse than attending a long (and usually boring) meeting when the chair you're sitting in is extremely uncomfortable.
- Flooring is also an important factor. Is crossing from the entrance door to the reception desk a pleasant experience? Do visitors get the 'red carpet' treatment, even if the floor is tiled?

Every tactile aspect of décor in a customer interface can be important, whether it's a handle on your showroom door or the plaster on your waiting room walls, so choose those things that align with your brand's values and personality.

And don't forget the all-important toilet facilities. Do you provide a typical noisy hand drier and bland paper towels – or are your customers treated to Egyptian cotton hand towels that are light and fluffy to touch? If you don't think it matters that much, try visiting one of the best-brand hotels in your area and experience the care its staff take over all the sense-of-touch opportunities they want their guests to experience.

A sense of touch on the web

Finally in this chapter, what about the internet? Is it really possible to put the sense of touch on to a website? I believe it soon will be. Even though the technique is still very much in its infancy, many research labs are currently engaged in finalising hardware and software that will put impressive tactile experiences into the hands of website visitors.

Touch-screen technology has advanced rapidly since its introduction in the 1970s. Our own domestic PCs, PDAs and satellite navigation systems have made extensive use of touch screens. Retail settings, point-of-sale systems, information booths, training rooms and ATMs have all incorporated a tactile user experience. (Have you considered how a touch screen might boost the sense of touch for your customers? You could provide an information point in your reception or showroom area or on your exhibition stand giving options to view various product or service details, look at advertisements, or listen to pre-recorded messages about your company.)

The real progress in regard to websites is occurring through *haptic technology*, which uses motions and vibrations fed through controllers to create a tactile user/computer experience. Examples of haptics that have been around a while are joysticks and game controllers, and some definitions of haptic devices would include mobile phones that vibrate when you have a message.

Perhaps the game controller represents one of the first opportunities to develop a tactile website. In a conversation I had with Ian Cocoran, author of the excellent book *The Art of Digital Branding*, he conveyed his excitement about the whole development of the sense of touch for the internet. In conversation with me, Ian said:

> **The concept of touch will be huge, as it brings yet another sensory dynamic into play for web users who are hell-bent on a daily fix of one brand or another. Imagine logging on to the website of your favourite sports car brand, for example, and simultaneously holding a gaming controller in your hands. A virtual test drive is waiting for your command to wave the starting flag. As the powerful beast roars around the track, you feel every judder as you enter each hairpin bend, and every gear change is experienced directly through your finger tips.**

A combination of stereoscopic imaging that creates 3D imagery is also being developed in conjunction with haptic devices to give an even greater sense of touch linking the user and the virtual world of a website. In place of a mouse, visitors to a website put a finger on the end of a robotic arm, which allows them to manoeuvre through the website. Inside the robotic arm, motors respond to the movement of the user's finger, creating a force against it. These reactions are picked up by the skin's receptors and enable tactile feelings to be experienced, including textures and shapes.

At the time of writing, these haptic units are not yet on sale, so we must look to other ways of incorporating touch on our websites. If there is no way currently to feel fabrics, surfaces and textures without some intermediary device, then the solution is to utilise additional delivery mechanisms. Let's return to our chopsticks example again. What if the chopsticks were mailed out minus the instructions for use, but with a card that directed the recipient to your website, where the instructions could be found? In this respect, your website visitors are engaged in both a visual and a tactile experience (just as they would have been if they'd received the instructions in the mailer), and both are intertwined. Granted, the *'feel'* part of the experience is not located on the screen. But it can still provide a tactile connection.

Now, what if we added some music on the website, playing in the background (Chinese music, perhaps)? How about if we incorporated the sense of smell into the mailing at the same time? What if there was a sachet of noodles as part of the contents, or a sachet of soy sauce? Suddenly we're moving from a single sense to employing all five.

And this is the key to building a powerful brand. In these last few chapters we've looked at all the five senses individually because we need to appreciate how each one has numerous opportunities for use in building a powerful brand. But when it comes to creating that total customer experience, none can work in isolation. It is the combined force of all the senses that makes up your most powerful brand weapon: your Brand Halo™. That is the subject of the next chapter.

5

Innovation

Innovation distinguishes between a leader and a follower.

Steve Jobs, co-founder and CEO of Apple

13

Building your Brand Halo™

Innovation can mean many different things, but in the context of building a powerful brand it's about finding new and better ways to deliver that all-important customer experience. It's a prerequisite for any brand that's going to avoid the short-term memory trash can and take up residence in long-term memory. In our fast-moving world, consumers get bored very quickly. The ground-breaking product or service that's grabbing attention today can become the stale, lacklustre norm of tomorrow.

Delivering your brand to the customer is therefore a matter of continual improvement, not a one-off exercise. It requires more than just putting together a collection of isolated activities, which is the way in which most businesses tend to operate. We've looked at the five senses in action and seen how they can all make a powerful contribution to your brand, but innovation must come from their *combined force* to have the desired effect. Don't misunderstand, however. Merely stringing the various components together so that all your ducks appear to be in a row was how many businesses approached the concept of integrated marketing communications – which often turned out to be a costly and futile exercise that had little going for it, especially from a sensory perspective. The only way you can achieve brand innovation in a cost-effective and productive manner is to have a system – one that not only defines each powerful, positive sensory encounter with the customer but does so consistently, year in, year out. It's a system that needs to be rigid enough to enforce and to discipline, but flexible enough to introduce new thoughts, ideas and developments into its framework.

That system is your Brand Halo™. It's the ultimate model for pulling all the elements of your brand activity together into the total customer experience. In this part of the book you'll learn how to create a Brand Halo™ that's unique to you and your business. You'll understand how each interface with the customer can be a time when your Brand Halo™ is polished or tarnished, depending upon what happens. You'll discover where your employees fit into the process, not as passive observers of a scheme someone else is responsible for, or as automatons merely functioning as the delivery mechanism, but rather as the ones who are totally involved in running, improving and advancing the customer experience. And you'll realise the importance of documenting all the key methods and systems that your business will use to ensure consistency in your overall approach.

The idea behind a Brand Halo™

Why is this system called a Brand Halo™? To answer that, we need to turn once more to psychology in order to provide the basis upon which the concept of the Brand Halo™ has been built. We've already seen throughout this book that the way we think can have a profound effect on our actions, especially when it comes to purchasing and branding decisions. Many of these thought processes are automatic, working at the subconscious level, so that we are frequently not even aware that we are in several respects being driven to buy a specific brand because of irrational and illogical emotional forces within our brain.

In psychology, various predispositions of this kind are grouped under the heading of 'cognitive biases'. One such bias, which often plays a major part in our decision making, is known as the *halo effect*, which is defined as follows:

The halo effect is the tendency to assume overall positive or negative characteristics in a person as a result of observing just one or two positive or negative characteristics.

In other words, if we meet a person who is good at A and B, we automatically think they are also good at X, Y and Z. Conversely, if we experience one or two negative things about someone, we are more likely to form a negatively biased opinion on their whole character. The old saying that 'you can't judge a book by its cover' may be true, but it's quite often the way we make our decisions.

It's wrong to stereotype people and hang labels on them, but typically it is what people tend to do. That's why the whole point about branding has to do with influencing perception, rather than rational thoughts, because the emotionally driven halo effect simply undermines our ability to be objective in making judgements.

One of the most common displays of the halo effect is a job interview, where the interviewer may dislike the interviewee's accent, dress or mannerisms. A negative bias towards the job applicant in even one of these areas may cause the interviewer to rate that person unsuitable for the position on all or most characteristics. Another example is that people who are seen as being physically attractive are often viewed as more intelligent, kinder and more successful than those who are unattractive.

This whole halo effect idea may seem somewhat far-fetched, but savvy marketers use it to great advantage. Celebrity endorsements of products and services are a classic example of exploiting the halo effect to boost sales. A celebrity who stars in a television soap as, say, a doctor can increase sales of all kinds of healthcare products and services by endorsing them even if he or she has had no medical training (and played a cop in another series). Celebrities can even give approval to products that have nothing to do with their television or radio characters, because their personality or lifestyle simply overrides any rational connection. They can even become self-professed experts in world affairs. It's not unheard of to find pop stars who suddenly become authorities on everything, including global warming and Third World issues – and most of the time they get a great deal more media attention than the 'real' experts.

The right parts of your business – but not all parts

The halo effect tells us something very important about our branding approach. It reveals that you don't have to get everything right, just certain parts that give the customers a favourable impression – one that's strong enough to carry your brand to their long-term memory banks. After all, do famous celebrities like Richard Branson, Tiger Woods or Oprah Winfrey get everything right, all the time? You must be kidding. One of the greatest baseball players in history, Babe Ruth, struck out more times than he hit the ball – but he hit it enough times for the halo effect to turn him into a legend.

What about Nike, Starbucks or IBM? Is their customer experience beyond improvement? Of course not – and they'd be the first to admit it. But there are enough plus points in their operation to generate a positive feeling about them. And that's the key to the success of your brand. *Put in place the most important customer experiences and the halo effect will do the rest, giving an all-round positive impression of your brand.* You know and I know that a totally perfect customer-oriented business does not exist and never will. But if you do just some of the right things in the right way, you'll be streets ahead of your competitors who still operate in a fragmented fashion. What's more, depending upon the depth and consistency of the positive experience, customers can be pretty forgiving about all those unfortunate errors that any business – including yours – will inevitably make.

This is the core concept of the Brand Halo™. You need to ensure that you are utilising every brand tool at your disposal so that the customer contact (or supporter contact if you are a charity) creates the most favourable impression that is possible – but not in every nook and cranny of a business, as some branding and management consultants would have you believe. That's an expensive pursuit, and one that the halo effect doesn't back up. Of course, if you can afford to decorate that old aircraft hangar you now use as an industrial warehouse with gold flake – even though your customers don't know it exists and will never set foot in the premises – then be my guest. But it won't really make any difference to the halo effect. Instead, you need to determine only the most critical times when your business and your customer connect with each other, and invest as much finance and resource as you possibly can on getting them to über level.

Customer contact timeline

In practice, all customer (and potential customer) contacts occur at one of three distinct times:

Pre-purchase – *raising awareness of your brand, product or service.* Typical contact times include:

collateral material	PR
website	point-of-sale material
conference	exhibition
sponsorship	salesperson
telephone	e-mail
weblog	text message
delivery vehicle	stationery (business card, letter)
clothing	TV/radio

During purchase – *ensuring the sale is progressing smoothly.* Typical contact times include:

product/service demonstration	e-commerce link/site
shopping cart	retail space
order confirmation	price list
face-to-face	shopping bag
product packaging	product/service instructions
delivery method	hospitality
travel/accommodation	tour of facilities

Post-purchase – *developing the relationship and maintaining brand awareness.* Typical contact times include:

follow-up paperwork/information	after-sales service
satisfaction survey/questionnaire	'thank-you' customer evening
invitation to event/show	text message
e-mail	sell-on product/service
free sample	referral/testimonial

For non-profits, you could consider these three phases in terms of:

- supporter identification (through raising awareness);
- supporter conversion;
- supporter retention.

Plot your contact times for your particular charity. Some of the above commercial examples will obviously not be appropriate for a non-profit enterprise, but many can still be applied.

Determining your key customer contact points

However many customer contact times your business has, we're only interested in the ones that are the most important. The question is, how do you know which ones they are? The answer is by plotting out a Customer Contact map.

If it sounds complicated, believe me it isn't. All you really have to do is to chart the journey your customer (or potential customer) takes from the pre-purchase initial contact with your business right through to the post-purchase follow-up stage. Break each leg of that journey into its separate contact points, then determine the *high-importance* and *low-importance* ones and identify them as either activities you are initiating (outbound contacts) or ones where your customer or potential customer makes the first move (inbound contacts). Questions you can ask that will help you to determine which contact points are key include the following:

1. What is the purpose of this particular contact point?
2. Who is it for (eg existing customer, lapsed donor, potential new client)?
3. How well does it work?
4. What are the processes involved (eg staff, software, hardware)?
5. How resource-intensive is it?
6. What would happen if this contact point didn't exist?

Once you've considered these points, you can plot the outcome using a simple two-axis scale, like the one shown in Figure 13.1.

Let's look at a pre-purchase stage Customer Contact map for Brookman Executive Recruitment as an example. Sharon Brookman runs a small recruitment business, which identifies potential candidates, conducts interviews and then selects the shortlist for presentation to the client. Sharon employs four other members of staff, two of whom help her with her brand activity, including general sales and marketing support.

Between them, they agree that most clients are generated by a small set of comprehensive brochures that are sent out on a regular basis. As this is a contact point that Brookman Executive Recruitment instigates, Sharon places it in the high importance/outbound quadrant. The business has also had a good response from articles written for various business magazines, and this is also placed in the same quadrant. As a result of these actions, clients

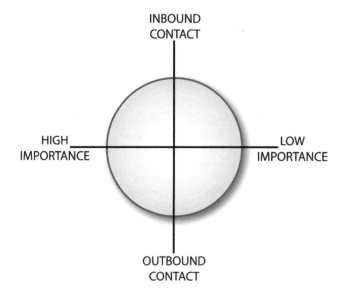

Figure 13.1 A simple two-axis contact point

telephone to arrange meetings with Sharon – an inbound contact that is of high importance.

At times, potential clients referred by an existing customer will call, and again this is classed as an important inbound contact. She usually travels to meet them at their own offices, so this is an outbound contact – and a pretty important one at that, thus gaining a place in the high importance/outbound contact quarter.

Sharon has tried other methods of raising awareness, including trade shows and advertising in directories, but these have only ever brought in a handful of enquiries, most of which did not lead to new business. She's also tried cold calling, which was found to be the least effective and the most time-consuming. Although the business has a website, the stats have never shown a particularly high hit rate, or response. So, these contact points are placed in the low importance/outbound contact part of the customer contact map.

The company rarely receives any e-mail or written enquiries from potential clients, so these can be considered inbound contacts of low importance. The result of this customer contact mapping is shown in Figure 13.2.

Just by carrying out this simple exercise, Sharon and her staff can see immediately the key areas of concentration for building the brand experience.

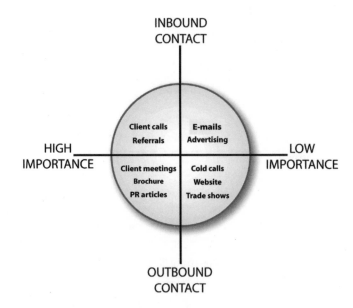

Figure 13.2 Sample completed contact point

They can also appreciate where considerable time and expense may have been invested for little or no return. This may sound obvious, but many businesses are quite happy to carry on wasteful activities in the hope they will eventually be rewarding, while at the same time doing little or nothing to improve those parts of the business that bring in the best responses.

Please don't misunderstand: it is not a case of neglecting to look after your customers at any time or place in your business – that must never happen. Rather, it's about being realistic and focusing on those areas where you – and your customers – stand to make the biggest gains. In an average small business, as few as three or four main contact points at each of the three stages (pre-purchase, during purchase and post-purchase) should give you enough opportunities to create an impressive Brand Halo™, but this will vary according to the nature and size of your operation, the markets you serve and the amount of financial and human resource you have available to invest.

If as a small business you try to incorporate too many contact points, you'll find it an unwieldy and costly process. As I've already said, the whole idea behind the Brand Halo™ is that you just don't need that many contact points on which to dedicate your resources, provided the ones you do include wow the customer like nothing else on earth.

Involve your employees

If you employ staff, they should be assigned the task of mapping your customer journey and identifying all the contact points en route, as with our Brookman Executive Recruitment example. (I'm assuming here that you have explained to your people what the concept of the Brand Halo™ is all about and followed the information in your Brand Storybook™, which you will learn about in the next part of the book.)

Once the entire journey is recorded and the key customer contact points in each stage of your business – pre-purchase, during purchase and post-purchase – have been agreed, break the group into smaller teams and assign them the responsibility of creating and delivering the brand experience at these points. If you employ only a small number of people, give each individual the accountability for all the selected contact points in a given stage – all those in pre-purchase, for instance.

Creating your Brand Reflections

Now comes the exciting part. At every single customer contact point you have designated, you need to create a Brand Reflection that overlays it.

A Brand Reflection consists of the following components that enable you to provide the most powerful emotional brand experience at that point in time:

- the five senses;
- your Brand Storybook™ (which we'll cover in Chapter 15);
- your Brand Lexicon;
- your foreground and background emphasis.

Every action performed at each customer contact point is accompanied by a Brand Reflection (see Figure 13.3). All actions are designed to elicit the highest emotional benefit for the customer and push the brand into long-term memory. You will use the five senses to create a total sensory experience. Your foreground and background will determine which elements of the Brand

SIGHT
SOUND
SMELL
TASTE
TOUCH
BRAND STORYBOOK™
BRAND LEXICON
FOREGROUND
BACKGROUND

Figure 13.3 A Brand Reflection: vital to your business

Reflection are emphasised and which are subdued, while your Brand Lexicon will ensure that the language spoken does not deviate from the agreed words and phrases that explain your product, service and brand. All of this is underpinned by your Brand Storybook™, through which you communicate your brand philosophy.

Note that a customer contact point (sometimes called a 'touchpoint' in other books and articles) is not the same thing as a Brand Reflection. I think it's important to separate the two. A customer contact point might only involve a particular electronic process, which of itself lends nothing to the brand. Overlay it with a Brand Reflection, however, and you have a whole host of sensory assistance to make that process part of your total brand experience. Removing the Brand Reflection doesn't take away the contact point or the process. A Brand Reflection is there to enhance, not to replace.

A Brand Reflection example

Let's return to Brookman Executive Recruitment and see how Sharon creates a very basic, but nonetheless impressive, Brand Reflection for one of her pre-purchase customer contact points: the client meeting. Of course, before

Sharon arrives at the potential client's premises there would probably be an outbound customer contact where Brookman Executive Recruitment would confirm the date and time of appointment, facilities, etc. This in itself is another ideal opportunity to create a memorable customer experience. But for this example, let's assume that this has been completed and Sharon is on her way to the meeting.

To begin, Sharon has first defined the emotional benefit that she wants to evoke as a result of this particular Brand Reflection. As the meeting is with a prospective new client, Sharon determines that a feeling of confidence in her company is the desired outcome.

Incorporating the five senses

Sharon then considers how the five senses can help deliver this. Visually, she can create specific materials for the meeting – a slide presentation, for example, with accompanying handouts. This presentation will contain embedded audio, so that the sound sense is also utilised. Of course, she is appropriately dressed for the occasion, ensuring that her outfit matches her brand culture and philosophy – another plus point for the visual sense. As for smell, Sharon always personally carries out presentations to new clients, so she wears a particular perfume – one that conveys an air of confidence without being overpowering.

The potential new client has provided tea and coffee, so Sharon begins the presentation by placing some branded mints on the table 'as an accompaniment to the drinks'. Throughout her talk, Sharon refers to specific parts of the handouts, which are printed on a textured surface that reflects an upmarket, confident feel. She makes certain that key words and phrases from her company's Brand Lexicon are used often throughout the presentation, and any technical words that the potential client might not understand are listed in the handout – right at the front, so the client doesn't need to feel embarrassed by having to ask what a particular word means.

In all of this, Sharon has made certain that the key elements of her presen-tation are emphasised (ie in the foreground) while other distractions are kept firmly in the background. Sharon always brings her own laptop and projector to meetings, because that way she is in total control of the circumstances. However, she doesn't want her laptop and projector cases cluttering up her presentation space, so she moves them underneath the meeting room table, out of sight. Neither does Sharon want various cables and leads to spoil the view, so she has made some small velvet-type fabric sleeves through which the visible cables can be fed. The sleeves, of course, are in her firm's colours, with 'Brookman Executive Recruitment' embroidered all the way down the sleeve. The client sees the impeccably dressed Sharon and the impressive visual materials – but doesn't see the cables or the other baggage.

The whole of Sharon's presentation is client focused. But intertwined with the emotional benefit she is offering and the supportive material that goes with it, she narrates her company story: why she started her business and what her passion is for the work she does and the clients for whom she does it. When Sharon leaves, every aspect of that particular Brand Reflection has been covered.

Is the potential client impressed? Would you be impressed? I'll leave you to consider that one.

A complete Brand Reflection

This was a single Brand Reflection at its most basic. There were literally hundreds of other ways to approach this particular customer contact point. Yet it contained some interesting ideas that, despite being small, could have a major effect in terms of winning the business and contributing towards that brand experience.

Now, some readers might consider little things like the covering up of cables to be totally insignificant. But that misses the point entirely. Branding, if you recall, is about getting your brand into long-term memory. That calls for doing something different or unusual, no matter how small. When was the last time you were in a meeting where the presenter covered up cables? Or handed out mints? I don't doubt for a moment that if such things had occurred among the myriad of typical 'same old thing' approaches, you'd remember it. And when you put that one Brand Reflection together with all the rest, you have the best opportunity there is to drive your brand forward.

But it doesn't stop there. After a time, Sharon's Brand Reflections at the various mapping points may become stale. Branding is not static; it is a dynamic process that requires continuous improvement, cutting out the things that don't work anymore and replacing them with new ideas and approaches. As Sharon's business grows, she might be able to afford the purchase of technology that allows her to give her presentation wirelessly, with full surround-sound. It may be upgraded to a DVD rather than a slide show, and she may get her client to become more involved in the presentation through tactile equipment. Changes of material, of textures and of smells will all keep the brand fresh over time. And, assuming Brookman Executive Recruitment wins the new client, the pre-purchase stage will move to the 'during purchase' phase, then the follow-on stage of post-purchase. All these will require continual brand development.

YOUR BRAND HALO™

Figure 13.4 Your Brand Halo™

When you have created a Brand Reflection for every customer contact point that you mapped, you simply join them together – and you have created your Brand Halo™. This holistic ring of sensory and emotional delivery encompasses your business to project a powerful brand every time in a constant and consistent manner. It is your Brand Halo™ that resides in the long-term memory of your customer.

> Your Brand Halo™ is the total of all your Brand Reflections that deliver the brand experience.

Every individual Brand Reflection that forms part of your Brand Halo™ is fully aligned with the rest. Your Brand Halo™ will be described in full via a Brand Halo™ Handbook that defines activity at each Brand Reflection in terms of people, brand processes and brand procedures. Each element will be described in detail so that there is always consistency in the way the customer experience is delivered. (We'll look at this handbook in more detail later.)

Do you see how this approach is different from merely attempting, in some fragmented fashion, to 'exceed expectations' or 'love the customer'? I've consulted for many small businesses over time that spent enormous amounts of hard-earned cash trying to put in place something that the customer never asked for and didn't want anyway. I've watched small business executives wine, dine and bestow gifts on potential clients, thinking that this abundance of generosity 'delighted the customer' and would therefore win the client, only to hear the line, 'Sorry, but I'm giving the business to one of your competitors. Good steak, though.'

Finding out some contact preferences

Building a powerful brand is all about creating the strongest positive perception in the minds of your customers. But your *existing* customers already have a perception – one that's the result of all the experiences over time they've had in dealing with your company and, if you employ staff, your people too. The only way to find out about their current perception is to ask them. But how you do it is very important. You not only want to discover whether they are happy with your service, but also need to know what, from their perspective, are the key contact points on your Customer Contact map.

Many smaller businesses carry out little or no market research, as cost is frequently a prohibiting factor. Some resort to handing out 'satisfaction cards' that ask customers to rate product features or service levels. All too often the feedback is very limited in what it says, and in the majority of cases the data sit in a filing cabinet drawer somewhere, never to see the light of day. I can't recall the last time a product or service was modified or improved because of something I wrote on a card.

Our questionnaire is aimed at obtaining some basic information about levels of satisfaction, but goes on to discover the broad sensory preferences your customers have when dealing with your company. The questions are based on an aspect of Neuro-Linguistic Programming (NLP) to do with what are known as *sensory modalities*, or representational systems.

Modalities: a preferred sense of contact

Here is what we understand. Although we utilise all the five senses when processing data, in any given context we will have a preferred sense – a modality – that will take the lead. NLP classifies people into three fixed types, a classification that we call the V–A–K model:

1. **V – Visual people**: those whose visual sense will dominate their focal point in a particular situation. They will make certain buying decisions based on how things look.
2. **A – Auditory people**: those who will use their sound sense as their focus when processing information. They prefer to hear about your product or service.
3. **K – Kinaesthetic people**: those who will utilise their sense of touch, taste and smell to process information, more than the other senses. They like to experience the product or service (touching, tasting, smelling) to determine whether or not to buy.

It is very important to understand that these are broad characteristics, and context dependent. I've heard many NLP trainers and coaches state emphatically that most people are '65 per cent visual, 20 per cent auditory and 15 per cent kinaesthetic', as though these states were fixed. That is an entirely erroneous statement, because it doesn't take into account context. For example, when you are out running, you are operating in a highly kinaesthetic state and it would be silly to suggest that your focus is entirely visual. When you are reading, your focus is visual, and listening to music is obviously auditory. The brain shifts from one modality to another depending upon context; however, it still remains true that in specific contexts a particular sensory modality will take precedence.

An auditory person reading a book while listening to music will be inclined to focus on the music more than the book. It is not unusual for that person to stop reading quite often in order to listen more intently to the music before returning to the book. Modality preferences have been evidenced in schools and colleges where studies have shown that instructional resources matching students' preferred learning modalities achieved higher test scores than the mismatched materials.

Focus on the major trends

Of course, we cannot alter the sensory focus of our Brand Halo™ to suit every single individual who does business with us. What we are looking for are the major trends. The 'Pareto principle', otherwise known as the '80–20 rule', states that 80 per cent of your business comes from 20 per cent of your customers. These percentages will vary but the ratio is usually about right. So, we need to find the perception factors that hold true for the majority of your customers.

The following, then, is a brand perception questionnaire for you to copy that incorporates sensory questions. Because businesses differ in the products and services they have to offer, you may need to modify the questions somewhat. You can also add your own questions, but don't make the questionnaire too long, or people will not want to take the time to fill it in. Although the questionnaire is quite unsophisticated when compared to professional market research studies, the results should at least indicate what kind of perception the majority of your customers have, and what 'lead system' they use to determine that perception – visual, auditory or kinaesthetic (V–A–K) – at certain contact points. You'll see that each sensory 'tick box' question follows the same V–A–K order.

Once you know the preferences, use the information to help build the Brand Reflections in your business. For example, if 70 per cent of your customers prefer to hear from you rather than see you in the context of announcing new products and services, the sense of sound (music, speech, earcons, etc) will be a bigger focus for you than visual material at that point.

Asking the questions

You can conduct this survey in a number of different ways. Sending a questionnaire through the post is perfectly all right. So is e-mail. Or, if you want to keep a regular check on your customers' perception of your business, create it on your website. The key to participation is to offer some incentive for taking part, where you can. It could be a small gift specifically chosen for those who respond, or you might give a discount on their next purchase of your product or service, or a reduced rate over a period of time. See how innovative you can be with your 'thank-you' to the responders.

Use this covering letter to accompany your questionnaire. Add your own information inside the square brackets.

Dear [*enter name of customer here*]

As the [*enter your job title*] of [*enter your company name here*], I want to thank you for being one of our valued customers. I want to ensure that we always serve you as best as we can, and so I'd appreciate it if you'd take a few minutes to tell me what you think about our business and its product/service [*delete as applicable*]. This information will be used to evaluate our level of customer satisfaction and help us plan our service offering for the future.

Please return this form [*or give alternative if sending via e-mail, or posting on the web*] by [*enter cut-off date*]. As a token of my appreciation for your helping us, I'd like to offer you [*state offer/ discount/gift here*] with my compliments. I look forward to hearing from you.

Kind regards

[*your signature*]
[*enter your name and job title here*]

PS [*use this PS where data protection laws apply*]
Please note that as part of our data protection policy, we will not attribute this information to any named individual when collating the results of this survey.

Questionnaire

From what you know about [enter your company name here], please answer the following questions and/or tick the relevant boxes:

1. What do you think [enter your company name here] does (in a sentence or two, please)?

_____

2. In thinking about the quality of service you have received from us recently, how did we fare?

❑ Extremely unsatisfactory
❑ Unsatisfactory
❑ Average
❑ Very satisfactory
❑ First class

3. If you indicated 'Unsatisfactory' or 'Extremely unsatisfactory', please could you tell us what happened?

_____

4. If you had cause to complain, how would you describe the way in which the situation was resolved?

❑ Extremely unsatisfactory
❑ Unsatisfactory
❑ Average
❑ Very satisfactory
❑ First class

5. Overall, when you deal with our company, what's most important to you? (Tick just one box, please.)

❑ The total image of your business.
❑ The way I'm spoken to by your staff.
❑ The way I feel I'm treated.

6. When we introduce new products or services, how would you prefer us to let you know about them? (Tick just one box, please.)

❑ Show you what they are through a brochure, mailer or your website.

❑ Tell you about them through a telephone call or visit by a representative.

❑ Provide a sample for 'hands-on' experience.

7. When I meet with people from your company, the most important thing to me is: (Tick just one box, please.)

❑ How they look
❑ What they say to me
❑ How they make me feel

8. What four (4) words from the following list would you use to describe [enter your company name here]?

❑ Sincere   ❑ Cooperative
❑ Competent   ❑ Organised
❑ Sophisticated   ❑ Systematic
❑ Open   ❑ Practical
❑ Conscientious   ❑ Creative
❑ Agreeable   ❑ Effective
❑ Reliable   ❑ Efficient
❑ Innovative   ❑ Punctual
❑ Successful   ❑ Friendly
❑ Intelligent   ❑ Polite

9. What makes [enter your company name here] different from other options available?

_____

10. What is the most important thing about [enter your company name here] – the thing that causes you to use [enter your company name here] over any other company for its product/service?

_____

Vive la différence

In 2007 the enlightened Harley-Davidson company named the women's market as its fastest-growing segment, citing an annual spend by women of around $300 million on Harley bikes in the United States alone – no small sum, especially as it even excluded Harley-Davidson accessories, riding gear and clothes.

Women today have a huge influence in buying decisions, can often be found at the helm of giant corporations and, thanks to their shrewd investments, have controlling interests in major operations throughout the world. Despite this, most businesses are still tending to treat target audiences as though they were all-male. In a UK survey conducted a couple of years ago it was found that 91 per cent of women felt that advertisers didn't understand them, despite the fact that a fifth of all media advertising was aimed at women rather than men. Marketing to women is a hot topic today, and businesses which assume that adding a few pink shades to their marketing materials or logo will suffice will be in the loser's seat very quickly. In order to include women successfully in brand strategies, we need to understand the ways in which they think differently from men.

If your business sells to a predominantly male or a totally female audience, then you have a clear line of demarcation with which to work and address accordingly. But what are the implications of reaching a target audience of both males and females when trying to create appropriate Brand Reflections? Much will depend on the kind of business you operate and the target audience you serve, but here are some overall considerations:

- **Men make purchasing decisions based on a shorter pay-back term than women.** Men generally buy products and services to gratify an immediate need, with less thought for the future. Women, on the other hand, are more persuaded to buy goods that will satisfy their needs over a much longer period of time. The longevity of a product may be a much stronger deciding factor than for men.

  Brand Reflection consideration: Use appropriate emotional cues for the two different sexes. Generating feelings of impatience and impulsiveness may get men to respond the most. Women may act in response to emotions relating to confidence in their purchasing decision and prudence in their choice of goods or services. Ensure that they understand the benefits of the product over the long term. This is a generalisation, though, as women with a large amount of expendable income may not feel so future oriented.

■ **Men justify their purchases with facts and data more than women, who operate at a deeper emotional level.** This doesn't mean that men aren't emotional; all decisions are made at the emotional level, regardless of gender. It's just that men like to use facts and data as a reassurance that they've made the right purchasing decision.

Brand Reflection consideration: Both sexes need adaptive or supportive emotional cues, but make sure that there are plenty of facts and figures for the men to study (even though information overload means they probably won't). At the same time, ensure that your Brand Storybook™ is in full force, as women will find emotive narratives ideal sensory cues for that deeper emotional experience.

■ **Men will make purchasing decisions based on a peer's referral, while women prefer to use their own past experience as a decision factor.** In other words, men are quite happy to purchase goods or services on the basis of a friend or colleague's recommendation. Women, on the other hand, will listen to other women's opinions but use this information as a support and will make their own mind up more independently.

Brand Reflection consideration: For the men, have plenty of testimonials and referrals available, and, where possible, use peers from the same 'tribe' or social group as endorsers of your product or service. For the women, you can still provide appropriate testimonials, but you can also generate feelings of independence and confidence in their own decision making.

■ **Men are greater risk-takers than women when purchasing online and are not website-loyal.** Women will take fewer risks and make more informed purchase decisions. When satisfied with an online brand, they will generally remain loyal to it.

Brand Reflection consideration: If you run an online store, you've two choices: either take the middle ground and give plenty of emotional reasons to both parties why they should trust your brand, or be creative and give your website two portals: one for men and one for women. You can then create some gender-specific pages that ultimately lead to the same shopping cart. The men's pages can feature a more carefree, fun approach to the purchase (depending on your product or service, of course) while the women's pages can take a more confidence-building and brand-boosting route. In both cases, make sure there are also significant offline Brand Reflections in order to build the brand.

- **Men usually study the trees, while women focus on the woods.** In other words, men are much more inclined to focus on the immediate purchasing surroundings as compared to women, who go for a broader picture.

  Brand Reflection consideration: Use interesting facts and figures to create important tangible product or service benefits for your male audience (but remember to be emotionally driven at all times). Use your Brand Storybook™ to its fullest extent to relate personal and professional values that women look for in their wider brand evaluation context.

- **Men build relationships through joint activities, whereas women build relationships by talking together.** The difference is most notable in sports activities, where men may speak very few words, yet team bonding can be strong. Women prefer face-to-face communication where they can find common interests and share experiences. They also engage with and understand body language more accurately than men.

  Brand Reflection consideration: Arrange branded hospitality events for your male customers (tickets to a match or taking part in a sports challenge). Your female audience may be interested, too, but make sure you also hold complementary networking or 'thank-you' evenings where women can have the opportunity to talk together.

It's important to understand and incorporate distinctions between men's and women's thinking into your Brand Halo™. If that sounds a daunting task, take comfort in knowing that there are far more similarities than there are differences and a great deal of information that's given out by pop psychologists is anecdotal rather than backed up by sound evidence.

If you are specifically wanting to gain a larger number of female customers only, then you'll need to study marketing to women in much greater depth (a good place to start is the excellent website www.rethinkpink.com). Otherwise, strive for a balanced approach at all times. The key to remember is that a sensory and emotional approach to branding works for both sexes. The rest is really fine-tuning.

14

Your Brand Halo™ Handbook

Ask any franchise operator to name one of the most important parts of his or her business and you'll always get the answer: the operating manual. This document defines and controls the manner in which the entire business must be run. Without an operating manual, corporations like McDonald's would never be able to replicate their outlets worldwide with such accuracy and consistency. In short, the operating manual defines the system and the processes that keep the whole business running like clockwork.

In similar vein, businesses today often operate a quality system in order to meet required standards such as ISO 9000. This, too, needs a well-documented manual listing the standards and benchmarks that assure consistency in the way the company is managed and its product or service delivered.

Your Brand Halo™ also has a system and processes that need to be delivered in a consistent manner, just like a franchise. That can only be done through written documents. If it's not written down, then everything is left to chance. It only takes a member of staff who hasn't been told what occurs at a particular Brand Reflection for your Brand Halo™ to be tarnished rather than polished because she or he was just winging it.

To maintain a consistent brand approach in your business, you need to create a Brand Halo™ Handbook. This document should cover all the details of the brand activities in your company and who is responsible for them. It also incorporates, as separate sections, your Brand Storybook™, your Brand Lexicon and, if you have one, your Visual Identity Manual.

Your choice of contents

The Brand Halo™ Handbook should provide a written description of what takes place at every Brand Reflection you have defined. Just how deep you go with your detail is your choice to make. Some companies will want to spell out everything over pages of text, whereas others may get by with a series of simple checklists. How your Brand Halo™ Handbook is put together (a four-ring binder or an electronic document) is not the important issue, as long as information can be updated by new developments.

What is vital is that the Brand Halo™ Handbook has enough information about each Brand Reflection to be an accurate guide to delivering and innovating your Brand Halo™ – and that it gets used, rather than simply gathering dust on the top of a filing cabinet somewhere. As a minimum, your Brand Halo™ Handbook should address all the points you covered when creating your Brand Reflection, including:

- who and what is involved in the Brand Reflection;
- how it is done – referring, if necessary, to other sections of the Handbook, such as the Brand Lexicon or Brand Storybook™;
- when it is done and under what circumstances;
- whether it is outbound or inbound;
- the desired emotional outcome.

There is no right and wrong way to list this information. It is best to keep it as short and simple as possible, but you do want to include enough information in order that any one of your staff, given training, will be able to refer to the manual and deliver a Brand Reflection to the required standard.

A sample page from the Brand Halo™ Handbook

Using our Brookman Executive Recruitment example from the previous chapter once more, let's take a leaf from Sharon's Brand Halo™ Handbook to see how the page details the Brand Reflection for that particular customer contact point. In this instance, Sharon has opted for a four-ring binder rather than an electronic version.

The first page of the Handbook contains a diagram of her Brand Halo™ that shows all the Brand Reflections in the three purchase stages. Each Brand Reflection is given a number so that it can be immediately identified. Then, each page of Sharon's Brand Halo™ Handbook acts as a detailed checklist pertaining to each element of the Brand Reflection. Referring to the sample page shown in Figure 14.1, let's go through the contents that are included.

- As you can see, the page begins by establishing which Brand Reflection it is referring to, using both its identification number and the purchase stage. The outbound/inbound designation has also been established. Every employee will have responsibility for delivering and innovating at least one Brand Reflection, therefore it's important that everyone knows who he or she is, and so this is listed next. As Sharon is the only one to carry out new business visits, her own name is recorded as the Innovator.
- Following on, all the five senses are identified, together with their corresponding details. Notice that the page refers to another section of the Handbook that covers dress codes in the company, as well as an audio reference (to a CD that is placed in a pocket at the back of the Handbook) and various storage cupboards located in the company's offices.
- Processes and systems involved will take place at all Brand Reflections. This page highlights the need to check the hotel booking confirmation, although on this particular occasion the potential client is just a car drive away and therefore a hotel booking isn't required.
- Equipment: a list of all the electrical equipment needed for the meeting and where it can be located.
- Scripts/prompts: businesses with a sales department or call centre may need telephone scripts or outlines as prompts for the sales executives. In addition, scripts or prompts that cover fixed-type presentations can also be written and copies included in the Handbook. This can be as a part of the Brand Lexicon's contents, or a section on its own.
- Finally, the foreground/background division is described, just as it was when constructing the Brand Reflection. The foreground refers to the cable covers listed under 'Equipment'.

BROOKMAN EXECUTIVE RECRUITMENT

BRAND REFLECTION 3: POTENTIAL CLIENT MEETING

Stage: Pre-purchase, Outbound

Brand Reflection Innovator: Sharon Brookman

EMOTIONAL BENEFIT:

To evoke feelings of confidence in company.

KEY SENSORY ACTIVITIES:

1. SIGHT:

Use new business brochures. Business suit (4) as shown in dress code section.

2. SOUND:

Use Brookman corporate music (audio folder, file 7) embedded in slideshow.

3. SMELL:

Personal brand signature scent.

4. TASTE:

Brookman-branded mints. Take from confectionery cupboard.

5. TOUCH:

Covered by business brochure textures.

PROCESSES/SYSTEMS INVOLVED

Confirm hotel booking if needed. Organise SatNav for directions. Ensure car is valeted.

EQUIPMENT

Laptop and LCD projector from equipment cupboard. Check loading of slideshow and all slides.

Use extension cables and two-way socket from electrical cupboard.

Use cable covers from main storage cupboard.

SCRIPTS/PROMPTS

Use standard new business script (2) from Lexicon.

FOREGROUND/BACKGROUND

Hide laptop and LCD cases.

Fit cable covers.

Figure 14.1 Brand Halo™ Handbook sample page

A Handbook for your business – and your people

Every employee should have a complete version of the Handbook. Your Brand Reflection innovators review their respective contact points and introduce new ideas and sensory approaches. After successful testing, the relevant pages are replaced with the updated versions. That way, your Brand Halo™ remains fresh and creative.

All of this may seem simplistic. But look at it this way. Imagine you work for Sharon's executive recruitment business. Once you've read this one page from its Brand Halo™ Handbook, what are the chances that with a little training and guidance (and knowledge of where the storage cupboards were), you could implement that Brand Reflection exactly as detailed?

Not only that, what are the chances that by referring to the Handbook you could deliver that particular Brand Reflection 10, 50 or 1,000 times – in a totally consistent manner? Now, what are the chances you could do it that well if you didn't have that checklist to go by? Delivering the total customer experience cannot be done by a 'seat of the pants' approach. It needs guidelines, management and discipline.

Creating your Brand Halo™ Handbook will give you all three. That's why it's a 'must-have' if your Brand Halo™ is to be the highly effective delivery mechanism of your total brand experience.

6

Communicating your brand

In the future, leaders will have to become storytellers first and managers second in the new society.

Rolf Jensen, *The Dream Society*

15

Your Brand
Storybook™

Are you sitting comfortably? Then let's begin.

Once upon a time, many thousands of years ago, our hunter-gatherer ancestors would end each day by drawing together around a campfire. After a hearty meal, with the fire still burning brightly, the main event of the evening would begin: storytelling.

Tribal members would wait with anticipation to tell their stories with passion and conviction. A recounting of the food-gathering activities and how the prey was tracked down by the proud hunter, or a lamentable tale about the fish that managed to get away. Vivid recollections of their surroundings, such as describing the majesty of the tallest trees or the brilliant colours of various berries picked that day.

These stories were rich in imagery, replete with actions, characters and events. Listeners would be enthralled as humour, excitement and imagination all merged to produce wonderful narratives that continued to be told well into the night. Diverse though the stories may have been, they all had one thing in common. They were the glue that bound the clan together in hope and expectation.

Stories are the oldest form of influence in our entire history. The National Storytelling Network says that, 'Stories are the building blocks of knowledge, the foundation of memory and learning. Stories connect us with our humanness and link past, present, and future by teaching us to anticipate the possible consequences of our actions.'

Without stories, human communication would be sadly lacking. We are hard-wired to experience the world through meaningful narrative. By sharing experience through stories, we transmit accumulated knowledge, wisdom, beliefs and values across the globe. And with storytelling, we do it emotionally, not just as dry facts and figures.

In today's society, technology has become the all-encompassing driver of information. Previously fragmented media options have been replaced by technology that joins together vast arrays of communication streams, flowing as mutually supported channels.

The digital revolution of today has learned from the former dotcom disasters and now, at the time of writing, its successor, web 2.0, is busily generating new technologies that will create a multitude of business and social networks of information, where customers, business partners and others are brought together. The rise of blogs, podcasts and sites like Facebook and MySpace is an example of how web 2.0 has already evolved. Mobile phones, PDAs and laptops are now 'old' technology. In the future the digital revolution will serve you even better. It will turn on your television when you get home without so much as a voice command. Your refrigerator will put itself online and order product refills when the stock gets low. There seems to be no limit to what technological advances will achieve.

The need for stories today

With so much information technology at our fingertips, together with an unbelievable freedom of choice, it seems crazy to think that customers would be interested in listening to stories, least of all from a business. But it's true. The digital revolution has given us so much, yet at the same time it has largely ignored the very basic need of everyone to be motivated, excited and inspired.

In his best-selling book *A Whole New Mind* (2005), Dan Pink states that:

> . . . the last few decades have belonged to a certain kind of person with a certain kind of mind – computer programmers who could crank code, lawyers who could craft contracts, MBAs who could crunch numbers.

> But the keys to the kingdom are changing hands. The future belongs to a very different kind of person with a very different kind of mind – creators and empathizers, pattern recognizers and meaning makers. These people – artists, inventors, designers, storytellers, caregivers, consolers, big picture thinkers – will now reap society's richest rewards and share its greatest joys.
>
> Dan goes on to emphasise that the brain's capabilities responsible for powering the information age are no longer sufficient by themselves to drive the future needs of the emerging world, but rather it is the 'qualities of inventiveness, empathy, joyfulness, and meaning' that will determine who flourishes and who flounders.

We've already seen from previous chapters that in this materially satisfied society, customers want meaningful dialogue with suppliers, not an endless wave of boring monologue built around facts and figures that no one cares about any more. They want a conversation with your business that's rich in all the symbols, metaphors, meanings and experiences every good story contains. If you can offer that kind of customer communication, you will be well on the way to creating a powerful brand for your business.

I can't emphasise enough that brands today are not separate entities from the rest of our lives. Rather, they are the guidance systems for who we are and how we live. The car we drive was once a mere status symbol, reflecting an earning capacity or demographic profile. Today, the car you drive and the clothes you wear define your lifestyle, ideologies, qualities and preferences. How can cold, hard facts and figures alone lead us to such emotionally driven choices? The simple fact is, they can't. We've already established that small businesses that compete only on a commodity platform (product, features and price) have a limited lifespan. But give customers a reason to believe – a story about your brand and how it relates to their lives – and you'll have the best chance of gaining a customer.

Brands are built around stories, and stories of identity – who we are, where we've come from – are the most effective stories of all. This is a powerful way to bring them to life.

(Bill Dauphinais, global leader for brand marketing and communications, PricewaterhouseCoopers)

In psychology, there's a saying: 'People who like you tend to be like you.' In other words, their values, beliefs and ideas are similar to your own, which leads to a natural bonding. Likewise, when your brand values are espoused through captivating stories, you can develop meaningful business relationships with customers who are in alignment with your particular credos, stance and worldview. And those are the customers you need to concentrate your efforts on.

In 2007, adidas launched its 'Impossible is nothing' campaign. Apart from its debut in the form of television commercials, it took in websites, print ads and documentaries, all aimed at encouraging everyone to take their first step in reaching their 'impossible' dream. The campaign featured stories of real people successfully attempting to overcome what had once seemed like insurmountable obstacles, and through their stories adidas hoped to inspire people to think about their own difficulties and how to overcome them.

More than 30 international athletes were asked to illustrate a critical moment in their lives, using their own hand-drawn illustrations and paintings. Here in the United Kingdom, the first one I saw featured David Beckham telling the story of how he faced death threats from fans after the 1998 FIFA World Cup. Another ad featured US basketball player Gilbert Arenas telling viewers why he wore the number zero on his shirt.

In all of this, I didn't see one product demonstration. I didn't get told about the quality of the material. No shots of the pattern on the soles of adidas trainers. No close-ups of the laces. And would I necessarily care anyway? But Beckham opened the ad by saying, 'I'm David Beckham and this is my story' (see Figure 15.1). On a day that was full of seemingly insurmountable obstacles, I listened to him talk about how difficult life can be sometimes, but how it's important to stay with it. Suddenly I was revived. If he could do it, so could I. The whole ad spoke to me. It was a story. Short, yes. But full of emotion. Told by a celebrity who is an international brand. A story that motivates, one that you internalise, one that you can buy into. Then (and only then) do you have the product shot in the very last frame.

Figure 15.1   A scene from the adidas 'Impossible is nothing' television commercial. Used with permission of adidas

Now, if you were broke and simply needed a pair of trainers to wear, you might go for whatever was the cheapest in the store. That's a commodity purchase dependent upon price alone, no brand required. Yet if you could afford it, you might just go for adidas. They'll cost you a lot more. That's OK, because you'll be willing to pay the extra. Not because of their superior construction, but because of how they make you feel. You put them on and immediately you are transformed into a sports superhero, dealing with adversity yet through sheer persistence coming through in the end. Your imagination is fired every time you don those trainers. They become a part of who you are... the part that believes 'impossible is nothing'.

Creating Your Brand Storybook™

Your Brand Storybook™ is the starting point for creating powerful brand communications. It contains four key components:

- your BrandMe™ story;
- your BusinessBrand™ story;
- your PeopleBrand™ story;
- your BrandBite™.

Each aspect of your Brand Storybook™ relates to a particular part of your overall brand. While the different elements are all important as individual branding devices, they should all be used holistically in order to create a powerful, cohesive brand message.

YOUR 'BRANDME™' STORY

Usage: Great for public relations, building awareness, creating differentiation from your competition and establishing an emotional bond with customers.

Your 'BrandMe™' story is, as the name suggests, a story all about you. In the sales and marketing professions the word 'unique' is probably one of the most overused words there is. Unfortunately, many small businesses fall into the trap of promoting their product or service as 'unique' when in fact there is very little that anyone can claim as being the only one of its kind today. As the saying goes, 'There's nothing new under the sun.'

However, there is one thing that is unique and will remain so: *you*. There isn't anyone else like you on the face of the earth! Not even your twin brother or sister can claim to be an exact replica of you in every single aspect of your life. You have your own life experiences, individual dreams, aspirations, ideas, opinions, beliefs and preferences. When you share some of these with your target audience in a relevant, interesting way, you will already be well on the way to standing out from the crowd. The key is to make them relevant to your business and your customers (and potential customers).

What kind of content should be in your 'BrandMe™' story? Here are some subjects and ideas that are always interesting:

- **Your history**. What has life's journey meant for you? Was your background one of poverty and deprivation, but through your determination you succeeded in becoming wealthy? The media in particular are always looking to publish stories that will inspire their readers. Think about the well-known celebrities and members of the rich list who started out with very little and ended up becoming famous.

  Perhaps you were already wealthy, but through circumstances you lost your money then started on the road back to success again. Many prominent figures today have often lost their money in the past then rebuilt their empire. Donald Trump, one of the United States' wealthiest businessmen and star of the US version of *The Apprentice*, lost his fortune in the 1990s but climbed back up to what is now reputed to be billionaire status. Rags to riches (and sometimes back again) is the perfect content for building great stories. But your story doesn't have to be built around adversity. You can instead create a story based on your travels, adventures, situations you have experienced, humorous times, difficult times – anything that will evoke strong emotional ties with your audiences.

- **Your mentors**. Who has provided the source of inspiration in your life? Family members, friends, teachers or coaches, or perhaps the people you most admire in the world, past and present? Great figures such as Mother Theresa, Gandhi or Nelson Mandela have given inspiration to countless men and women who saw in them qualities they admired, and desired to have themselves, whether it be succeeding against all odds, having a disciplined mind, living with honesty and integrity at the highest level or reaching a particular level of accomplishment. If they are qualities you have sought after and applied in your business, then you have a story to tell.

■ **Your achievements**. What have you done in your life that's worth telling others about? Many small business operators fail to acknowledge that even by starting their own companies they have achieved what for many is just a dream. Bill Gates, considered the world's richest man, began his business in his garage, as did Jeff Bezos, the founder of Amazon.com. It took Sir James Dyson, another wealthy entrepreneur, 10 years and countless rejections from major manufacturers before he was able to launch his world-renowned cyclonic vacuum cleaners. The achievements of many business icons of this calibre have created great stories for the media, and most have gone on to feature in autobiographies, giving their brands even more 'personal power' (as well as extra revenue from book sales and royalties).

Tell your story as though you mean it

Of course, whatever story you tell must be told with passion and conviction. The audience, whether a magazine reader scanning an article about you or a potential client listening to your presentation, must believe in you. If you attempt to 'con' the audience by making false claims or paying only lip service to what you claim to believe in, they'll spot it in an instant and your brand will suffer.

Today's customer is street-savvy. We've all heard the empty promises companies make. We've all read the unbelievable company mission statements, engraved on a wall plaque in a corridor or reception area somewhere, that make all kinds of attractive claims yet attract only dust and spider's webs.

If you want to stand out from the crowd, you have to walk the talk, and nowhere is it more critical than in your BrandMe™ story. Be honest and transparent, or they'll know for sure. As Ralph Waldo Emerson said, 'Who you are speaks so loudly I can't hear what you're saying.' Don't make the mistake of not being genuine.

YOUR BUSINESSBRAND™ STORY

Usage: A powerful way to establish an emotional connection with customers. Can be incorporated into sales presentations, business plans and proposals, as well as collateral material.

Now we extend the personal brand aspects into your business. The question this story needs to answer for your audience is: what does your business stand for? The chances are that if you asked a dozen of your customers right now, you'd most likely get a dozen different answers. So, you need to create a consistent, emotive and responsive story that brings out the best points of your business.

Unlike the typical corporate vision, which is often based upon sales revenue, growth strategy or product/service development, this story is about how your company operates: its ethics, responsibility, and connection with customers, and how it aligns with their wants and needs. This is the chance for you to get your customers (or, in the case of a charity, your donors and supporters) on board because they are of the same mind. This story will be one of involvement, something your ideal customer will find stimulating, involving and interesting.

The reasons behind your brand

Let's begin by asking why you started your small business in the first place. Was it because you were fired and had no other job aspirations, so you started up on your own? Was it because you thought you could make or supply something better than what was on offer? Did you have moral reasons for creating your company, or were they purely financial?

In 1975 a young woman by the name of Anita Roddick needed a livelihood to support her two children while her husband was away. Through her earlier travels around the world she had been inspired by cosmetic and beauty products from many different cultures, so she decided to open a shop selling moisturisers made from Bedouin recipes and sold in inexpensive plastic bottles. The shop was located between two funeral parlours, and the 'factory' was her kitchen.

From the very start, Roddick had a passionate belief in ethical consumption and business. She states that the products were sold on the stories that were behind them: emotive pleas for issues such as non-animal testing and human rights. Dame Anita Roddick (who sadly died in 2007) had a passion for fair trade and she developed the BusinessBrand™ story to go with it. As a result, her Body Shop grew from humble beginnings to a global corporation and was sold to L'Oréal in 2006 for £625 million.

Taking a stand for your brand

Could you justifiably claim to be morally, ethically or socially more responsible than your competitors because of your company's view on issues such as employee treatment, working conditions or supporting the local community? Some big-name labels selling trainers, T-shirts and other popular sports items have been accused of manufacturing their premium-priced branded goods in Third World sweatshops where low wages, poor conditions and child labour are rampant.

If you were a small business making similar items, what story could you tell that might gain a sympathetic ear from customers disillusioned by alleged bad labour practices? If it's relevant to your business, what are you saying about fair trade and green business issues? Consumers are becoming more ecologically aware and turning to those companies that can present an emotive case for sensitive issues such as fair trade, organic farming and sweatshop-free production.

In 2006, Cone (www.coneinc.com), a strategy and communications agency engaged in building brand trust, released the results of its Millennial Cause Study, which explored how corporate cause-related initiatives influenced millennials (those born between 1979 and 2001) as consumers, employees and citizens.

From a sample of 1,800 respondents, which comprised 895 males and 905 females between the ages of 13 and 25, the findings were eye-opening:

■ Eighty-three per cent stated that they would trust a company more if it were socially/environmentally responsible.

- Seventy-four per cent were more likely to pay attention to a company's message when they saw that the company had a deep commitment to a cause.
- Sixty-nine per cent said they considered a company's social and environmental commitment when deciding where to shop.
- Eighty-nine per cent said that they were likely – or very likely – to switch from one brand to another (price and quality being equal) if the second brand were associated with a good cause.
- Sixty-six per cent would consider a company's social and environmental commitment when deciding whether to recommend its products and services to others.
- Moreover, the poll found that as millennials began to enter the workforce, they had high expectations not only of themselves but also of their employers. Nearly 8 out of 10 wanted to work for a company that cared about how it contributed to society, while more than half said they would have refused to work for an irresponsible corporation.

As Carol Cone, chair and founder, stated:

Corporations need to align their brand with a cause that is relevant, authentic, sustainable and engaging, as well as one that is true to the core brand identity. Most importantly, companies cannot be afraid to communicate their cause commitments with honesty and sincerity. Millennials want to know how their support of a specific brand or product is actually making a difference.

There is every reason to expect that teenagers and young adults in the United Kingdom reflect similar statistics.

(Thanks to Cone for permission to reproduce these 2006 Cone Millennial Cause Study findings.)

Service with a stance

If you are in a service business, what are the equivalent concerns? What is different – even controversial – about your stance on matters relating to your profession? For example, a team-building and management training company in the United Kingdom took the view that other training companies were too quick to go into a client's company, carry out a predetermined training programme, then leave without due regard for the individuals in the team. So, it offered its clients a six-month follow-up programme with telephone and one-to-one support for all the members of the team it was training. Its managers believed passionately that every single individual in a team needed personal development at some level, and wanted to ensure that everyone had an equal opportunity to improve his or her performance. In the words of the team training business owner, it wasn't just about earning fees. It was to do with the 'buzz' the company trainers received at seeing someone develop skills and leadership capabilities, especially as a result of the added value the team-building business was providing.

With appropriate PR and presentations that emphasised the passion and drive to improve team-building standards, the business became enormously successful. Of course, each trainer was a skilled professional and therefore the product was good; but the owners agree that without the BusinessBrand™ story, they might have been mixed in with all other team-building companies when trying to approach potential clients.

YOUR PEOPLEBRAND™ STORY

Usage: Deliver your PeopleBrand™ story in your recruitment process – in advertisements, recruitment literature and as part of the interview process. Then make sure the PeopleBrand™ story is upheld on a continual basis.

How much do your staff, if you employ any, really know about you and your business? Do they feel like mushrooms (kept in the dark and fed on you-know-what), or have they got such an in-depth understanding of what you do and why you do it that they come to work each day with a passion to drive the brand forward?

Many companies, despite often repeating the worn-out phrase 'our people are our business', are lost when it comes to delivering their brand through employees. But think about this. If branding is all about engaging with the customer at the emotional level, isn't it pretty obvious that your people should also be emotionally aligned with the brand as well? After all, how can they convey the appropriate brand perceptions to the customer if they don't know what they are themselves?

Surveys conducted in both the United Kingdom and the United States show that companies where employees understand and buy into the brand story can expect up to a 30 per cent greater return on their staff investment than other firms. At the same time, in companies that have a typical cliché-ridden mission statement, as many as 75 per cent of their workforce don't think they do business in the way the mission statement describes. The huge Enron energy company's mission statement boasted that 'We treat others as we would like to be treated ourselves. We do not tolerate abusive or disrespectful treatment. Ruthlessness, callousness and arrogance don't belong here.' After Enron became the world's biggest bankrupt corporation in 2003 amid allegations of scandal and corruption, copies of the company's mission statement became best-sellers on eBay as people clambered to own a copy of Enron's meaningless rhetoric.

Your PeopleBrand™ story should be written using the same emotive, passionate type of content as your BrandMe™ and BusinessBrand™ stories. After all, if customers are emotionally driven rather than rationally driven, your own people are no different.

Essentially, your PeopleBrand™ story needs to address the three key criteria for successful staffing: *attraction*, *selection* and *retention*.

Attracting good candidates

Why should anyone want to work for you? What do you have to offer that's better than your competitor down the road?

At one time, recruiting was mostly about what prospective employees could do for your business. Today, as society and culture have moved towards a brand-driven framework, it's much more about what you can do for them – if you want to attract the best possible staff for your business and your brand, that is.

Employees, like customers, have perceptions and preferences, and are more inclined to look for roles where the business aspirations align with their own. If you can't match them, the chances of your even attracting the right kind of potential candidates are slim. How do we know what those preferences are? Generally, candidates perceive a desirable place to work as having at least the following four essential criteria:

1. *The business is successful.* This doesn't mean that your business needs to be big. Remember, it's the strength of the brand, not the size of the company, that counts. Therefore, your story needs to include the compelling parts of your BrandMe™ and BusinessBrand™ stories, which will show not only that the business is alive and well but that it also has a great future, which, naturally, candidates will want to be a part of.

2. *The work is interesting.* Even menial, repetitive tasks can be interesting, can't they? While human resource management is beyond the scope of this book, think about ways in which you have incorporated new ways of working to make things more interesting and enjoyable for your people. For example, if you operate a factory or assembly line, are you still in the dark ages of clocking in, one worker per task and strict to-the-minute breaks, or have you modernised your factory-floor production systems? Wherever you have innovated in your business, include that in your story – not the specific methods you've used, but rather why you've used them, what made you change, what you plan to do in the future.

3. *There is scope for learning and career progression.* Again, your story shouldn't be about the process or details of career paths; that's something to be discussed as part of ongoing human resource management in your business. What your story should convey is the opportunity for staff to develop personally and professionally at any level. How passionate are you about developing people? What limits do you place on your staff's ability to be successful? How will you help them get to where they want to go?

When desktop publishing (DTP) was first introduced, secretaries and personal assistants suddenly found boxes of software and manuals on their desks with notes from their bosses saying that DTP was going to save the company a lot of money on printing and design, so here was a chance to learn new skills. That was often the extent of their induction into the new technology and the limit of their training.

4. *There is a sense of innovation and a chance to 'make it happen'.* Will your business make the best use of the skills and talents that are within each and every member of the workforce? Will they be allowed to innovate so as to improve systems and procedures, and will they be given the responsibility and accountability to introduce new methodologies into your business? What emotive story will you present to show them how you fully intend to support and facilitate their hopes and aspirations?

Remember, your story does not have to be a tear-jerker, neither does it have to have would-be candidates rolling in the aisles with laughter. What it does have to be is *authentic*. So, if you and your company tend to be reserved and somewhat introverted, then don't go out to make people laugh. Remember, people who like you (and want to work for you) tend to be like you. Conversely, if your company is more extrovert and has a 'fun' approach to work, there is nothing wrong with using humour to good effect.

When Sir Richard Branson started Virgin Atlantic, he was ridiculed by the head of American Airlines, who said, 'What does Richard Branson know about the airline business? He comes from the entertainment business.' But this was a distinct advantage for Virgin. Sir Richard, a 'rebel' who 'stood for the people', built his story on the premise that 'work should be fun' and has gone out of his way to avoid the stuffiness of huge, faceless corporations. This somewhat quirky, entertainment-led approach permeates all of Virgin's communication to its customers.

Even during flights on Virgin Atlantic, the fun-loving cabin crew are apt to lighten up an otherwise dreary (but important) safety demonstration by saying, 'There may be fifty ways to leave your lover, but there are only four ways out of this airplane.' When coming in to land, it's not uncommon to hear the pilot say, 'We'd like to thank all of you for flying with us today. And the next time you get the insane urge to go blasting through the skies in a pressurized metal tube, we hope you'll think of Virgin Atlantic.'

What about salary?

Notice that throughout these key points I haven't mentioned money. There's a good reason for this, one that parallels the difference between a brand and a commodity. If the main incentive for a candidate is money, then for that candidate the brand is less important. Can you risk weakening your brand by hiring that kind of person? You can't afford to turn your recruitment process into a street market, any more than you can create a gilt-edged brand by price bargaining.

Of course, people have to eat, so salary needs to be discussed, as do job title and where the position will be located. But it's not uncommon to find candidates who are personally aligned to the business philosophy who are willing to take salary cuts and move long distances just for the opportunity to work with a winning brand. That is why such subjects are simply part of the contractual discussions, not components of your story.

Now that you have your story prepared, you can begin to utilise it as the basis for communicating throughout all of your recruiting channels such as recruitment pages, online recruitment websites and job fairs. Whether you use an external supplier to design and produce your recruitment ads and materials, or do it yourself, the key is to use the essence of your story and ensure that it doesn't lose its emotive strength along the way.

Figures 16.1 and 16.2 show how a company's brand character can be communicated through humour while still retaining its 'serious' side.

Selecting your potential employees

Assuming you've had responses to your recruitment campaign, invite all the candidates you feel fit the bill (having eliminated all those who clearly don't fulfil your basic criteria) along to a group meeting before you start interviewing individual applicants.

This is your opportunity to deliver your story seminar-style to all the hopefuls and get their reaction to what you have to say. Even if your business is large enough to employ a human resource executive or manager, this is one presentation that you definitely need to front – because it's your story that you want to tell.

The objective of your storytelling at this stage is to give everyone in the room the most accurate idea possible of what working for your business will be about. It's important that your own passion and belief come across with

Spoon-feeding, tantrum-soothing, bottom-wiping. And that's before I go on maternity leave. Wendy Pitches, PA to Iain Graham

THEY SAY a newborn baby is a big shock to the system. Me? I'm looking forward to the peace and quiet.

Don't get me wrong, this job's terrific and I fully intend to come back to it.

Graham Technology is an award-winning, fast-growing global company with a refreshingly different attitude.

My boss, the founder and Chief Executive, is energetic, enthusiastic and hugely intelligent. He also has a great sense of humour. (How else would I get away with this advertisement?)

But on the downside, he's eccentric, demanding, temperamental and at times downright infuriating.

So don't apply unless you have the patience of Florence Nightingale and the energy and resourcefulness of Cherie Blair.

Just like motherhood, it's a dirty job but somebody's got to do it. And at least you get to hand him back at the end.

Please apply in writing to: Wendy Pitches, Graham Technology plc, Torr Hall, Torr Road, Bridge of Weir, Renfrewshire, PA11 3RU.
e-mail: wendy.pitches@gtnet.com

Graham Technology

Figure 16.1 This highly successful recruitment advertisement, like the one shown in Figure 16.2, both by Edinburgh-based 60w Communications, introduced an emotive feel to what was formerly dry and purely factual narrative. Reproduced with permission

Figure 16.2 Communicating a company's brand character through humour: another example. See also Figure 16.1

sincerity and conviction, because all too often candidates take a job only to discover quickly that the actual position in the company isn't anything like how it was described at the interview! So, tell your story, and this time add detail about what you would expect from the successful candidate. Go through any specific job requirements, things that you feel strongly about in terms of accountability, discipline and character. Don't pull the wool over their eyes; tell it like it is. And when you've told them, give those who don't think they'd fit in with your business the chance to leave with no bad feelings.

After you have delivered your story, ask for questions and answer them honestly. If your story has done its job, those remaining in the room are the candidates you can then go on to interview separately.

Retaining your people

Hiring good people is one thing. Keeping them is something else. Why is there a huge turnover of staff in most small businesses? All too often it's because the story that was told during the attraction and selection process has become seriously diluted or was a clear case of misrepresentation. The problem is, one disenchanted employee can kill your brand faster than anything else – especially if that member of staff is on the front-line customer-facing duty.

Your PeopleBrand™ story not only should be a compelling introduction to your business but should be maintained and sustained throughout the life of the company. While a brand is not a promise you make to your customer, it's a promise you've already made to your employees – and one that needs to be permanently kept. Recounting the early days of Starbucks, Howard Schultz, chairman and CEO, says in his book *Pour Your Heart into It* (1999):

> **The only way to win the confidence of Starbucks employees was to be honest with them, to share my plans and excitement with them, and then to follow through and keep my word, delivering exactly what I promised – if not more. No one would follow me until I showed them with my own actions that my promises were not empty.**

But there is something else that's vitally important if your people are to carry the brand forward in their hearts and minds as well as their actions: make them a part of the story. No brand can ever stand still. The very fact that society and culture change over time means that your brand must keep pace with what's happening. Never lose the fundamentals of your original story, but innovate and add meaningful content, using your people as the source.

For instance, when you launch a new product or service, there's a story to be told. Why did you create this new item? Which of your staff were involved – and are involved – in the process of making or delivering it? What are their views? Are they excited, motivated, passionate about what it's going to do to help customers? What would they say about it if you invited them to a discussion over lunch? Did they work through the night, or at weekends, to get the product onto the shelves, or the new service delivered through the relevant channels? Was there any one particular person who was the 'hero' in its development? Any product or service is rich with content if you look for it.

Your employees can help you to formulate the story, add their own personal take on some or all of its content and emerge as an even more dedicated and committed group because they have an active part in that aspect of your brand.

YOUR BRANDBITE™

Usage: Provides the platform for creating an effective strapline, for dealing with telephone and e-mail enquiries and as the basis for creative advertising and promotions. Also vital for networking, and pitches to potential investors.

If you met someone who asked, 'What do you do?', how would you respond? Most business owners usually answer in a very predictable manner. They say, 'I run a widget company', 'I sell XYZ', 'I'm a landscape gardener' or 'I'm an accountant'. Even executives in not-for-profits are prone to say, 'I'm the CEO of St Abraham's Hospice', as though the listener is already totally familiar with their valuable work. All these answers have one thing in common: they are usually given in terms of what their job is, or what duties they perform.

The problem is, describing your profession in this way means that the listener has no idea of what you really do or, more importantly, how you can provide a solution to a customer's problem. In the absence of information, people will usually resort to what they can remember, or what they already assume is true. Thus, if you say that you own an accountancy firm, you haven't defined your service as being of any benefit. If the person who asked the question has a worldview that accountants are nothing but expensive bookkeepers, guess what's just happened to your chance to communicate the value of your business? That's right, it's just disappeared.

We've already seen that people do not buy features, they buy benefits – and emotional ones at that. So, when you get the opportunity to describe what you have to offer, the last thing to do is reel off some meaningless dialogue about your product, service or company. This is especially true if you are involved in a business that provides complex goods or services that are hard to understand. 'My business provides ninge-wheel boggit springs for heavy-duty compressors.' Duh... describing your business or what it does in pure functional terms is a guaranteed way to halt the conversation. Very few, if any, customers can make the leap (or be bothered, even if they could) between what you do and what it means to them.

On the other hand, if you turn the question to your advantage and respond with an answer that gets their attention, you have a much better chance of opening up the dialogue.

In the past decade or so, an increasing number of businesses have sought investment from venture capitalists and business angels. But these people are very busy and don't appreciate time-wasters. So, they need to hear a short, succinct description of the business idea and the potential rewards it offers to the backer. This demand has given rise to the idea of the '30-second elevator pitch': getting your point across concisely as though you were in an elevator with a potential backer and had just the journey to the investor's floor in which to grab the investor's interest. Not-for-profit executives also need a good BrandBite™. Meeting potential supporters and financial donors at a function means an opportunity to explain face to face what you do. If you can't articulate your message in a concise and attention-grabbing way, you may not get another chance.

I didn't have time to write a short letter, so I wrote a long one instead.

(Attributed to Mark Twain)

Like an elevator pitch, your BrandBite™ is a concise statement about the emotional benefits someone receives on using your product or service. Your BrandBite™ is purposely brief because its function is to get attention and interest so that further questions are asked. In other words, it's the primer, not the whole message. On the other hand, it's not a strapline either (even though it is a good basis for the development of a strapline), so 'Just Do It' won't do.

Here's an example of how to turn a description of your business offering into a BrandBite™. My good friend Terri Bodell runs a life coaching and psychotherapy practice in London. It would be very easy, when someone asked her, 'What do you do?', to answer, 'I'm a life coach'. Huh? What's that? Who knows? Worse still, Terri could say, 'I'm a therapist who uses the Ericksonian approach to behavioural modification.'

Yeah, right. Like, that's so interesting.

Instead of these non-starters, Terri says, 'I help people to get from where they are to where they want to be in life, in the shortest possible time.'

Notice that Terri has mentioned the kind of people she works for (people who want to move forward) and at the same time created an emotive hook – but hasn't yet described in any detail exactly what she does or how she does it. However, the listener could already be trying to imagine what Terri meant. Does she deal in financial success (rags to riches), or maybe she helps people move house? Perhaps she provides a service for singles looking to find a partner? The point is, it's a statement that leads to curiosity, because it has aroused interest. When tried on 12 listeners, all of whom were unknown to Terri or to each other, the kind of responses they gave were questions such as, 'That's interesting. How do you actually do that?', or 'I know where I'd like to be. Can you help?', or 'Wow. What kind of work do you do?' Each response was a request for more information, which is exactly what your BrandBite™ is meant to encourage.

Make use of metaphors

Depending upon the kind of business you operate, it's not always possible to be overly vague yet still provide enough emotive content to create interest. The key is to construct your BrandBite™ around the value that you bring to the customer, and then use emotive metaphors to enhance what you're saying. In other words, what's important to the customer from an emotional benefit viewpoint? Getting back to the accountant we mentioned earlier, instead of saying, 'I run an accountancy firm', how about 'I help people like you keep more of their hard-earned money by showing them how to pay less in taxes.'

Here are some key points about creating your BrandBite™:

- **Keep it simple.** No MBA language, in-speak or technical jargon. One way of making sure your BrandBite™ is crystal clear is to tell it to some 10-year-old children and see if they understand what you're saying.

- **Emotion is not the same as hype.** Hype belongs in empty, meaningless mission statements, not in a BrandBite. So, phrases like 'maximising performance', 'totally cost-effective', 'unique approach', 'next-generation' and 'leading-edge' are old and cold. We've all heard them so many times before that they have lost all meaning. If your business is able to improve a company's performance, what is the emotional outcome of that? Remember, performance improvement is a functional benefit but it's not an emotional one. There has to be something beyond the improvement that the customer envisions. What is it? Freedom? The ability to sleep at night? A frustration-free work situation?

- **Point out the difference between you and your competitors – but do it emotively and don't mention any specific rival.** Think back to Anita Roddick's concept for The Body Shop. Her BrandBite™ could have been, 'We create beauty, but unlike others we don't do it at the expense of human rights and animals suffering.' Or what about an electric boat builder, who might state, 'We build boats for messing about on the river without messing up the environment.' Corny, perhaps, but infinitely more memorable than, 'We build electric boats that work on a rechargeable battery system rather than using a petrol [gas] engine.'

- **Use similes and metaphors.** Similes are an easy way for customers to remember your products or services, especially if they are detailed or rather technical. Similes describe what something is *like*, only they do it with gusto and emotion. If someone says, 'Fred went about it like a bull in a china shop', you know exactly how Fred behaved, without the need for further explanation. Superman could be described as having 'superior aerodynamic velocity', but it's much more memorable – and effective – to say that he's 'faster than a speeding bullet'. If you were offering broadband services to internet customers, which would be the better BrandBite™: talking about megabytes and gigabytes, or using similes such as 'connecting you at lightning speed'?

  Metaphors are also great for use in a BrandBite™. While similes generally use the words 'as' or 'like' when making a comparison, metaphors make a direct connection by stating that something *is* something else, not just like it. For example, a business operating a take-away coffee bar could use the BrandBite™, 'We brew coffee that's Brazil in a cup.' Or if you run an online recruitment service, you could say, 'We provide a website that's a window on the job world.'

Creating a slogan or strapline

When you have a completed BrandBite™, you have a short, pithy and emotive 'taster' of what your business is all about. A BrandBite™ should be less than 50–100 words; the shorter it is, the better and more effective it will be.

But even that is too long for use in an advertising campaign, or as part of a piece of collateral. Customers are bombarded with thousands of marketing messages every day and remember very few. So, it's important to give them something to take away that's easily remembered and at the same time provides a hook to the overall message that you want to get across. That is where a good slogan can help to reinforce your company message. Advertising slogans (or 'straplines', as they tend to be called in the United Kingdom) accompany all the successful brands, from Honda's 'The Power of Dreams' to Microsoft's 'Where do you want to go today?'.

Most business slogans are like the worst mission statements ever constructed. Banal and meaningless, they include statements such as, 'Solid, sound service', 'We never say no' (but I suspect customers might), 'A better deal for you', 'The finest XYZ in the world', 'Quite simply the best' and so on. We've already covered the need for any part of the Brand Storybook™ to convey emotional benefits, so sorry, these just won't do.

One way to cut down your BrandBite™ into a slogan is to use our metaphor friends, because they give you the chance to be brief but creative. For example, one of the most famous slogans ever to be written was 'A diamond is for ever', the strapline of De Beers Consolidated Mines used in a print advertisement in 1948. (Since then it's been copied as a title for a James Bond film and the theme song that accompanied it.) Or how about 'It's everywhere you want to be', the strapline used in a long-running advertising campaign for a credit card called Access. Then there's the famous UK Hamlet cigars slogan, 'Happiness is a cigar called Hamlet'. If you notice, each of these slogans has an emotional benefit attached to it – something that is desirable, romantic or satisfying. As Samuel Johnson, one of England's greatest literary figures, stated, 'Promise, large promise, is the soul of an advertisement.' That promise must be one of emotional benefit – and should be evident in your strapline, whether it's subtle, metaphorical or in-your-face.

A UK storybook success

The storybook of innocent drinks, based in the United Kingdom, was bound to be a winner from the start. In the summer of 1998, three Cambridge graduates – Adam Balon, Jon Wright and Richard Reed – bought £500 worth of fruit and turned it into smoothies, selling them from a stall at a music festival in London. Their business mission was threefold: to make only 100 per cent natural products, to procure all ingredients ethically and to use ecologically sound packaging materials.

In less than 10 years, innocent have become the fastest-selling smoothies in the United Kingdom, with a 72 per cent share of the market, and still growing. Their turnover has spiralled to around £100 million and their ethical and moral business stance has garnered a host of dedicated followers – not to mention a string of top awards acknowledging innocent's values, business and marketing acumen.

Today, innocent's BusinessBrand™ story incorporates the Innocent foundation, a grant-giving charity that works in partnership with community-based projects. Every winter, innocent – with the help of supporters all over the United Kingdom – raises money by knitting tiny woolly hats to put on the tops of its smoothie bottles and donates part of the sale proceeds to help elderly people. In 2007 the target number of hats was 400,000. In addition, innocent has hosted a festival in London's Regent's Park every year as a way of thanking its loyal customers, with the proceeds going to a number of not-for-profit organisations.

The brand identity of innocent reflects its light-hearted brand character. Fruit Towers, its headquarters in London, is AstroTurfed throughout, and some of the vehicles used by the company are covered in grass and daisies (see Figure 16.3), while others have horns, eyelashes, udders and a tail.

Equally impressive is innocent's PeopleBrand™. As co-founder Richard Reed says:

> When it comes to employing people, we start at the beginning. We treat people the way we'd like to be treated ourselves, and we keep

things personal. If you get a job at innocent, your offer arrives with a case of drinks. Once the legal bit is over, we send you a little handbook that tells you all about life at Fruit Towers. And we make sure we give you a ring in the month before you join, just to say 'hi' and make sure everything is OK. We've found it's the little things that are appreciated best, such as having flowers on your desk when you arrive, and a nice little timetable that maps out your first two weeks. We also give people a pack of photos of the people they'll be working with and a map of the office, so they can recognise and find their new mates. But the bit that innocent people remember about their first few days is the 'lunchmate'. In your first two weeks, you are scheduled a series of lunch dates with all sorts of people, so you get to find out the office gossip and make a bunch of new friends. No more sitting in the local park on your own nibbling at a sandwich on a bench because you don't know anyone yet.

Figure 16.3 Co-founders of innocent drinks, Adam Balon, Jon Wright and Richard Reed and one of their 'dancing green vans'. Other photo: tiny woolly hats cover the innocent bottles

For more information on Innocent drinks, visit Innocent's website at www.innocentdrinks.co.uk. All material is reproduced with the permission of innocent.

Final thoughts

We've reached the end of our EPIC™ journey. From learning about what a brand really is, we've progressed through the various stages of emotion, perception, innovation and communication. We've seen how Brand Reflections can serve up the optimum customer experience and how, linked together, they form a powerful Brand Halo™ around your business.

Some aspects of branding may have seemed daunting, and parts of the psychology theories perhaps a little dry, but I hope that, overall, the information in this book has inspired you to start building a unique brand for your business from today. There's a great deal of practical information and ideas in these pages that you can begin to incorporate almost immediately.

I've been involved in advertising, marketing and branding for almost 30 years. During that time, numerous ideas, models and approaches have been offered to companies as the 'ultimate' solution to attracting new customers and being successful. Many of these ideas have fallen at the first hurdle. Others, though, having stayed around longer, are now way past their sell-by date and do little, if anything, to help promote a business in the 21st century.

I believe passionately, however, that sensory and emotional branding is here to stay. After all, if our customers – and potential customers – experience the world in which we live by their senses, doesn't it follow that to engage as many of the senses in our branding activity as we can will thus ensure greater success?

If you'll forgive the pun, it makes perfect sense to me.

Your Brand Halo™ is unique to your business. None of your competitors will have exactly the same Brand Reflections, Brand Storybook™ or even Brand Lexicon. In this way, your brand truly is an exclusive statement about your business – and as long as you keep your Brand Halo™ polished, it will shine for a very long time.

I'm reminded of a story regarding a group of tourists who were walking through the streets of a little Indian village. All of a sudden they noticed an old man picking up what appeared to be a scrap of wood. With a small rusty knife he proceeded to carve out the most beautiful miniature elephant. No sooner had he finished one than he scooped up another old piece of wood and carved another, then another. Amazed at the speed and accuracy of this old man, one of the tourists could stand it no longer. Walking up to him, she said, 'Excuse me, but I simply have to ask you, how are you able to take a very old piece of wood and with a rusty knife carve some of the most exquisite elephants I have ever seen. How do you do it?'

The old man paused for a moment and, looking her straight in the eye, he smiled and said, 'It's simple, really. I just cut away all the bits that don't look like an elephant.'

If you want to promote your business, attract customers and stand out in the marketplace, you need to cut away all the parts that don't look like your brand. And replace them with a Brand Halo™ that not only looks like your brand but sounds like it, tastes and smells like it, and feels like it, too.

If you take the leap and decide to implement the Brand Halo™ model in your business, why not let me know how well you're progressing? Or if you need help at any stage, I can provide you with coaching, training and in-house seminars. You can contact me at james@brandhalo.co.uk, or visit my website at www.brandhalo.co.uk.

Good luck with building your brand. I look forward to hearing about your success in the not-too-distant future.

References

Chapter 1   Just what is a brand, and who is the customer?

Morgan, G (1988) *Riding the Waves of Change*, Jossey-Bass, San Francisco
Winkler, A (1999) *Warp Speed Branding: The impact of technology on marketing*, John Wiley, Hoboken, NJ

Chapter 2   Branding the heart as well as the head

McCarthy, E D (1989) Emotions are social things: an essay in the sociology of emotions, in *The Sociology of Emotions: Original essays and research papers*, ed D D Franks and E D McCarthy, pp 51–72, JAI Press, Greenwich, CT
Reeves, R (1961) *Reality in Advertising*, Knopf, New York

Chapter 4   Perception and long-term memory

Frijda, Nico H (1988) The laws of emotion, *American Psychologist*, **43** (5), pp 349–58
Keller, K L (1987) Memory factors in advertising: the effect of advertising retrieval cues on brand evaluations, *Journal of Consumer Research*, **14**, 316–33

Kempen, L A C M van (2004) Are the poor willing to pay a premium for designer labels? A field experiment in Bolivia, *Oxford Development Studies*, **32** (2), pp 205–24

Chapter 9   Putting your brand on the right track

Milliman, Ronald E (1982) Using background music to affect the behavior of supermarket shoppers, *Journal of Marketing*, **46** (Summer), pp 86–91
North, A C, Hargreaves, D J and McKendrick, J (1999) The influence of in-store music on wine selections, *Journal of Applied Psychology*, **84**, 271–76

Chapter 10   The sweet smell of brand success

Hopkins, T (1983) *How to Master the Art of Selling*, Grafton Books, London
Lindstrom, M (2005) *Brand Sense: How to build powerful brands through touch, taste, smell, sight and sound*, Kogan Page, London
Proust, M (1982) *Remembrance of Things Past*, vol 1, *Swann's Way*, trans C K Scott Moncrieff and T Kilmartin, Vintage, New York

Chapter 12   Brand touch and feel

Cocoran, I (2007) *The Art of Digital Branding*, Allworth Press, New York

Chapter 15   Your Brand Storybook™

Jensen, R (1999) *The Dream Society: How the coming shift from information to imagination will transform your business*, McGraw-Hill, New York
Pink, D H (2005) *A Whole New Mind: How to thrive in the new conceptual age*, Cyan, London

Chapter 16   Creating your Brand Storybook™

Schultz, H (1999) *Pour Your Heart into It: How Starbucks built a company one cup at a time*, Hyperion, New York

Index

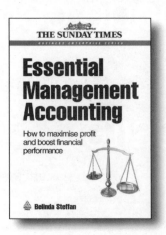